The New York Times

LITTLE HOLIDAY BOOK OF
MINI CROSSWORDS

The New York Times

LITTLE HOLIDAY BOOK OF MINI CROSSWORDS:
150 Easy Fun-Sized Puzzles

By Joel Fagliano

ST. MARTIN'S GRIFFIN ❧ NEW YORK

ISBN 978-1-250-19822-8

First Edition: October 2018

10   9   8   7   6   5   4

The New York Times

LITTLE HOLIDAY BOOK OF
MINI CROSSWORDS

Looking for more Easy Crosswords?

The New York Times

The #1 Name in Crosswords

Introduction

When you think about it, crosswords are particularly well-suited for our fast-paced, modern age. Almost every clue and answer is on a different subject, your mind bounces from one thing to the next, and when a puzzle's not too hard, it takes only a short time to do.

Well, if regular crosswords are modern, *The New York Times*'s new Mini crosswords are hypermodern. The clues and answers are just as diverse, but each 5×5-square grid takes a mere minute or so to complete—even less once you get good. You now feel the rush of excitement in finishing a puzzle in a fraction of the time!

Launched in 2014, and originally available only digitally, the Mini has become so popular that now on weekdays it also appears in print in the main section of the paper.

Each Mini is created by Joel Fagliano, the paper's digital crosswords editor, who started selling regular crosswords to the *Times* when he was seventeen. To date he's had more than 50 weekday and Sunday crosswords published in the paper, becoming in the process one of the most popular and accomplished puzzlemakers.

Joel packs his Minis with lively vocabulary, modern references, and the sort of playfulness and intelligence you'll find in its big brother elsewhere in the paper. The Minis are easy/medium in difficulty. The cultural references skew young. But don't let the small size and big squares fool you. These puzzles are decidedly for adults.

On the following pages are 150 Minis from the *Times,* lightly re-edited for their first publication in book form.

Let the many rushes of excitement begin!

—Will Shortz

	¹	²	³	⁴	
⁵					
⁶					⁷
	⁸				
	⁹				

ACROSS

1 Sound from a donkey
5 Freezing point of water on the Celsius scale
6 Orangutan doctor in "Planet of the Apes"
8 Country south of Ecuador
9 Toy on a snow day

DOWN

1 Sound from a bee
2 Harvests
3 Disney character with a seashell bikini top
4 "___ one to talk!"
7 French for "south"

2

	1	2	3	4
5				
6				
7				
8				

ACROSS

1 Lose one's footing
5 Khaki-colored cotton
6 In-between state
7 "___ the Earth Move" (Carole King hit)
8 Returning soldier's affliction, for short

DOWN

1 Key below Caps Lock
2 They're green when they're ripe
3 Words sometimes added to the end of a fortune cookie fortune for humorous effect
4 Game that starts with a break
5 Bit of video

ACROSS

1 Symbol in the center of a Scrabble board
5 Fashion's _____ Boss
6 Fragrant purple flower
7 "Bearded" flower
8 Johnny of "Pirates of the Caribbean"

DOWN

1 Hobbits' home, with "the"
2 Flower associated with Holland
3 Showing shock
4 Hip-hop's _____-A-Fella Records
6 Pot top

4

¹	²	³	■	■
⁴			⁵	⁶
⁷				
⁸				
■	⁹			

ACROSS

1 See here?
4 "Take a chill pill!"
7 Collection of Facebook photos
8 Reproductive part of a fungus
9 Pale and sickly-looking

DOWN

1 Cenozoic and Mesozoic, e.g.
2 Alternative to Zagat
3 Macaroni shape
5 Enveloping glow
6 Marvel Comics heroes

ACROSS

1 Fashionable
4 Words to live by
6 It's good for a laugh
7 Singer with the 2015 album "25"
8 Kylo ____, "Star Wars: The Force Awakens" villain

DOWN

1 Macho dudes
2 Someone you look up to
3 Opening for a dermatologist
4 Burn a bit
5 Like talking during a movie

6

¹	²	³	⁴	⁵
⁶				
⁷				
⁸				
⁹				

ACROSS

1 Channel for political junkies
6 Maker of the RLX, MDX and TLX
7 Things sold at Ollivanders in the Harry Potter books
8 Poet who created J. Alfred Prufrock
9 Criticize sharply

DOWN

1 Made a harsh birdcall
2 Richter or pH
3 ___ Wars (Rome-Carthage conflicts)
4 Intense passion
5 Mean-spirited

ACROSS

1 They're discussed in the Second Amendment
5 Get-out-of-jail money
6 Part of a flight
8 Jane Austen novel that "Clueless" is based on
9 New Year's resolution for losers?

DOWN

1 Muscles that benefit from crunches
2 Assigned stars to
3 Home of baseball's Marlins
4 Oozy stuff
7 Maze-running animal

8

ACROSS
1 Road deicer
5 With 6-Across, genre of the podcast "Serial" or Capote's "In Cold Blood"
6 See 5-Across
7 Hinged door fastener
8 Lambs' mothers

DOWN
1 Building material in "The Three Little Pigs"
2 Spring up
3 Take your ___ (suffer punishment)
4 Casual shirt
6 Friend of Fidel

1	2	3	4	
5				
6				7
	8			
	9			

ACROSS

1 With 9-Across, N.F.L. playoff round
5 Europe's neighbor
6 Tugs hard
8 Per diem
9 See 1-Across

DOWN

1 Wrong ___ (street sign)
2 Newton with laws
3 Grammy winner Ronstadt
4 Capital of Senegal
7 Pink Floyd guitarist Barrett

10

		1	2	3
4	5			
6				
7				
8				

ACROSS

1 Downed
4 "Oops, I ___ again" (Britney Spears lyric)
6 "Dreams From My Father" author
7 "Fifty Shades of Grey" author E.L. ___
8 Surgery sites, for short

DOWN

1 Douglas who wrote "The Hitchhiker's Guide to the Galaxy"
2 A metronome keeps it
3 Greek H's
4 Martial arts school
5 Letter-shaped construction beam

	1	2	3
4 5			
6			
7			
8			

ACROSS

1 African snake
4 "SNL" creator Michaels
6 Encourage
7 ☹
8 Number of lords a-leaping

DOWN

1 Noble gas that makes up almost 1% of the Earth's atmosphere
2 Possible cause of school cancellation
3 Ivy League school in Philly
4 ←
5 Fairy tale villain

12

ACROSS

1 Grabbed a chair
4 Frighten
6 Pixar film
7 Pyromaniac's crime
8 Part of the U.S. intelligence community

DOWN

1 Dip for a chip
2 Singer Guthrie
3 Many a Snapchat user
4 Ugly duckling, eventually
5 Pixar film

1	**2**	**3**	**4**	
5				**6**
7				
8				
	9			

ACROSS

1 Congressional decrees
5 Liquor, slangily
7 He sings "Rubber Duckie, you're the one"
8 Bill de Blasio, for one
9 Olympic swimmer's assignment

DOWN

1 Throat-clearing sound
2 Salmonesque color
3 Notorious skater Harding
4 Descendant
6 "___ we go again!"

14

	1	2	3	4
5				
6				
7				
8				■

ACROSS

1 Ump's outstretched-arms call
5 With 7-Across, "Space Oddity" singer
6 "Don't worry, you're ___ friends"
7 See 5-Across
8 Impertinence

DOWN

1 Striped Girl Scout cookie
2 Declares frankly
3 The end
4 Helpful kind of piece for a jigsaw puzzle doer
5 Applies with a cotton ball

ACROSS

1 Target of a swatter
4 Flannel shirt pattern
6 Python whiz, e.g.
7 Running total
8 What Theodore may be called

DOWN

1 Root beer and ice cream treat
2 Soup scoop
3 Triangular road sign
4 %: Abbr.
5 Like the American West, recently

¹	²	³	⁴	⁵
⁶				
⁷				
⁸				
⁹				

ACROSS

1 Sit around and waste time, with "off"
6 Airplane section where passengers sit
7 Do penance
8 "See ya later"
9 Shower with praise

DOWN

1 Suffix with land or moon
2 Condom material
3 "I'm on ___" (The Lonely Island song with the lyric "I got my swim trunks, and my flippie-floppies")
4 ___ de Mayo
5 Be in the front row in a team photo, say

	1	2	3	4
5				
6				
7				
8				■

ACROSS

1 Comic ____ (typeface)
5 Tycoon
6 California's Santa ____ racetrack
7 Tattered and torn
8 Picture of health?

DOWN

1 A school might be found using it
2 Heartburn
3 Like a professor played by Jerry Lewis and Eddie Murphy
4 Kill, as a dragon
5 Any brother in "Duck Soup"

18

	1	2	3	4
5				
6				
7				
8				

ACROSS

1 Fish whose name also means "complain"
5 Antisocial type
6 Pond buildup
7 Actress Ringwald of "Pretty in Pink" and "The Breakfast Club"
8 Big night for a high school senior

DOWN

1 Word before television or commentary
2 ___-Saxon
3 Kingdom
4 Field mouse to a red-tailed hawk, e.g.
5 Genie's home

	1	2	3	4
5				
6				
7				
8				■

ACROSS

1 Alternative for those who hate the 1%?
5 Taking out the trash, for example
6 Sorkin who wrote "Steve Jobs"
7 Be very popular on Twitter
8 "Sounds good!"

DOWN

1 "Jaws" creature
2 North _____ (nation in the news)
3 Humor form loved by hipsters
4 Repair
5 "Elder" or "Younger" Roman statesman

ACROSS

1 Where SpongeBob lives
4 "This is the worst!"
6 Place to store gold for a pirate
7 A golf course has 18
8 Put away the dishes?

DOWN

1 Process, as ore
2 Lack of difficulty
3 Aardvark's diet
4 Muscle malady
5 "That's crazy, dude!"

ACROSS
1 Not sweet, to a wine drinker
4 Reasons to bring in the National Guard
7 Japanese automaker
8 Hop out of bed
9 "For ___ a jolly good fellow"

DOWN
1 What RuPaul dresses in
2 Risotto or jambalaya ingredient
3 It's "wasted on the young," per George Bernard Shaw
5 Opposite of false
6 Gullible ones

22

	1	2	3	4
5				
6				
7				
8				■

ACROSS

1 Wynton Marsalis's genre
5 Party game with words you're not allowed to say
6 ___ acid (protein builder)
7 Disney World attractions
8 Watermelon eater's discard

DOWN

1 Foxx of "Django Unchained"
2 Tolerate
3 Like most urban land
4 Places with exotic animals
5 Blackens, as a road

ACROSS

1 Berkeley school, familiarly
4 Damage beyond repair, as a car
6 Carried
7 With 5-Down, director who boycotted the 2016 Oscars
8 Put into words

DOWN

1 Homes for hens
2 Heart chambers
3 Like Abe Lincoln, in physique
4 "Conan" channel
5 See 7-Across

24

1	2	3	4	■
5				■
6				7
■	8			
■	9			

ACROSS

1 Bookings for bands
5 All over again
6 Bone-muscle connector
8 "The Daily Show" host after Stewart
9 Perry who played the Super Bowl halftime show

DOWN

1 Pedal next to the brake
2 Confident way to solve print crosswords
3 Italian birthplace of Christopher Columbus
4 Worry about, in slang
7 "How come?"

1	2	3	4	5
6				
7				
8				
9				

ACROSS

1 Insurance giant with a duck mascot
6 "Top Chef" channel
7 "Objection, Your ___!"
8 Hall-of-Fame shortstop Smith
9 Uses a Kindle

DOWN

1 Hate, hate, hate
2 Stopped dead in one's tracks
3 Acclaimed tenor Mario
4 Steer clear of
5 Apple centers

26

	1	2	3	
4				5
6				
7				
	8			

ACROSS

1 Morning times, for short
4 Cancel on plans at the last moment, in modern lingo
6 Chef's wear
7 Vertically challenged, to put it nicely
8 Lead bug in "A Bug's Life"

DOWN

1 First Greek letter
2 "WTF with Marc ___" (popular podcast)
3 Hybrid garment for women
4 Musical notes after mis
5 Treelike creature in "The Lord of the Rings"

27

	1	2	3	4
	5			
6				
7				
8				

ACROSS

1 With 5-Across, it isn't played at home
5 See 1-Across
6 Pop music's ____ Brothers
7 1998 animated bug movie
8 NASDAQ competitor

DOWN

1 Ecstasy's counterpart
2 Desires
3 Knock the socks off
4 Thumbs-up
6 Artist Vermeer

28

		1	2	3
4	5			
6				
7				
8				

ACROSS

1 QB Newton
4 I.D. card feature
6 Chopt or Tender Greens specialty
7 Part of a Powerpoint presentation
8 2,000 pounds

DOWN

1 _____ Jost, co-host of S.N.L.'s "Weekend Update"
2 Just slightly
3 Pie à la _____
4 "Hey you . . . over here!"
5 Popular Xbox video game series

	1	2	3	4
	5			
6				
7				■
8				■

ACROSS

1 Swimmer's count
5 ___-B: dental brand
6 Really turned on
7 Sci-fi saucers
8 Hard to recall

DOWN

1 Shower sponge
2 ___ con pollo (Spanish dish)
3 Variety of violet
4 Cunning
6 "Whadja say?"

30

ACROSS

1 Triple ___ (Cosmopolitan ingredient)
4 Google Maps in book form, basically
6 Effective building material in "The Three Little Pigs"
7 Comic strip about a shopaholic
8 Tiny

DOWN

1 Ineffective building material in "The Three Little Pigs"
2 Upper echelon
3 Stashed supply
4 "The View" network
5 Where to see a vapor trail

31

	1	2	3	4
5				
6				
7				
8				■

ACROSS

1 01011010 or 10101100
5 Additive to coffee
6 Within the ___ of possibility
7 At 5 a.m., say
8 Manhattan-based designer label

DOWN

1 Start of a billiards game
2 Long (for)
3 Add up
4 Award for "Game of Thrones"
5 Street ___ (respect)

ACROSS

1 Steph Curry and Kevin Durant, for example
5 They're extracted from peanuts, coconuts and olives
6 Gas company that merged with Mobil
7 Clicked "I have read all the terms and conditions," usually
8 ___ Health magazine

DOWN

1 Gumption
2 One of Santa's reindeer
3 Trudges along slowly
4 Nine-digit ID
6 Sturdy tree

ACROSS

1 Au ___ (how roast beef might be served)
4 Philly Ivy League sch.
7 "You gotta be kidding me!"
8 Pointy-hatted garden statue
9 Ping-Pong table divider

DOWN

1 Founder of analytic psychology
2 Atop
3 Attach, as a button
5 It's found on the back of a jersey
6 Russian refusal

34

ACROSS

1 Playwright Shepard
4 Santa ____ (city where Super Bowl 50 was played)
6 Conceals
7 D sharp equivalent
8 Tina with a spot-on Palin impression

DOWN

1 With a heavy heart
2 Region
3 Sail supporter on a ship
4 Many a Food Network personality
5 "Tell me, what is it you plan to do / with your one wild and precious ____?": Mary Oliver

1	2	3	4	5
6				
7				
8				
9				

ACROSS

1 Communication device that beeps
6 Get away from
7 Time on the throne
8 Something controlled remotely?
9 Follows, as advice

DOWN

1 Capital city of Western Australia
2 Pain reliever brand
3 False front
4 Double-___ sword
5 Most Monopoly properties have six different ones

36

ACROSS
1 Clichéd Father's Day gift
4 Northernmost borough of New York City
6 Potato pancake
7 Gives approval for
8 Do stuff?

DOWN
1 Final tally
2 Black as night
3 Awkward people to run into on the street
4 Jezebel, for one
5 ___ over the coals

37

ACROSS
1 Volcanic emission
4 Froot ___ (cereal)
7 Sound heard before "Gesundheit!"
8 Head case?
9 Dairy farm sound

DOWN
1 "Regrettably . . ."
2 It may lose its mate in the laundry
3 Yawn-inducing
5 Game played on horseback
6 Millennium Falcon pilot in "Star Wars"

38

	1	2	3	4
5				
6				
7				
8				

ACROSS

1 Thing in an ashtray
5 Capital of Vietnam
6 With 7-Across, writer who said "I can resist everything except temptation"
7 See 6-Across
8 Chills in a champagne bucket

DOWN

1 Fundamental
2 Jeb Bush, to Jenna and Barbara
3 Warty amphibians
4 Where the rubber meets the road?
5 TV's "____ Met Your Mother"

1	2	3	4	5
6				
7		■	8	
9		10		
11				

ACROSS

1 Postal ___ (what the two-letter answers in this puzzle are)
6 About 71% of the earth's surface
7 The Granite State
8 The Peach State
9 Shrink in fear
11 Le ___, France

DOWN

1 Spiral shell
2 Women's golf star Lorena
3 The First State
4 Itching to go
5 Part of a drum kit
10 The Mountain State

40

	1	2	3	4
	5			
6				
7				
8				

ACROSS

1 Phenom
5 _____ Park, home to University of Chicago
6 Marketing connection
7 _____ Domini
8 Something to rap over

DOWN

1 Moan and groan
2 Animal in "The Lion King"
3 Birdbrain
4 School of Buddhism
6 You might pick it up at a bar

ACROSS

1 The "m" in E = mc^2
5 2015 theater award for "Hamilton"
6 Vampire vanquisher
7 Result of a mosquito bite
8 Questions

DOWN

1 Big name in applesauce
2 Taken ____: startled
3 Members of a Punjab sect
4 "What did I tell you?"
6 One-named pop star with the 2014 hit "Chandelier"

ACROSS

1 Vehicle that often has a miniature TV
4 Wing it
6 Lady Gaga's instrument
7 Gas gauge extreme
8 Crosses (out)

DOWN

1 Applauds
2 "___ Too Proud to Beg" (hit for The Temptations)
3 Hip-hop fan, in old slang
4 Tiptop
5 It's smaller than a penny

1	2	3	4	■
5				6
7				
8				
■	9			

ACROSS

1 Mouthful of tobacco
5 Posting on a store window
7 Biggest democracy in the world
8 Like frat parties and airport runways
9 Decomposes

DOWN

1 It rests on a violin
2 Pay tribute to
3 Sound portion of a broadcast
4 Something to keep a watch on?
6 "Oh yeah, ___ who?"

ACROSS

1 Rebounds or runs batted in, for short
5 Lowly chess piece
6 BB-8 in "Star Wars," e.g.
7 Chess piece used in castling
8 Sour bluish-black fruit

DOWN

1 Thread holder
2 Forbidden
3 Came to
4 "We know drama" cable channel
6 B&O and Reading: Abbr.

1	2	3	4	5
6				
7				
8				
9				

ACROSS

1 Things found on the back of Snapple caps
6 French ___ soup
7 Eskimo's shelter
8 Move stealthily, like a cat
9 Make fun of

DOWN

1 Force (upon)
2 Each one in a square is 90°
3 Tiny hairs that help paramecia move
4 Bugs Bunny and Scooby-Doo, for example
5 Evil Supreme Leader in "Star Wars: The Force Awakens"

46

	1	2	3	4
5				
6				
7				
8				

ACROSS

1 Alcoholic drink at a sushi bar
5 Like Wiccans and Druids
6 Revise, as the Constitution
7 Broadway honors
8 Not fancy at all?

DOWN

1 American ____ (U.S. territory in the Pacific)
2 F.B.I. operative
3 Rapper with the album "The Life of Pablo"
4 Split ____ (hair problem)
5 Trail in the woods

47

	1	2	3	
4				5
6				
7				
	8			

ACROSS

1 Univ. aides
4 With 6-Across, 2016 presidential hopeful
6 See 4-Across
7 "SNL" staple
8 Suffix with north or south

DOWN

1 Brownish gray
2 Ann ____, Michigan
3 Descendant . . . or a Toyota brand
4 "Here's to you, ____ Robinson"
5 Punch-in-the-gut reaction

48

ACROSS

1 Wile E. Coyote's go-to company
5 Stand-in
7 Carbo-loader's option
8 Give the cold shoulder
9 Refinery waste

DOWN

1 Smartphone downloads
2 Casino dice game
3 Major Iraqi city controlled by ISIS from 2014-17
4 When repeated, cry before "Read all about it!"
6 Opposite of yin

49

ACROSS

1 Warty amphibian
5 Accord automaker
6 ___ gas law (much discussed during Deflategate)
7 Gas meter, for one
8 "Don't believe the ___"

DOWN

1 When procrastinators don't do things
2 Outdo
3 "Honey catches more flies than vinegar," e.g.
4 Chip's chipmunk friend
5 Stoned

ACROSS

1 Aware of the way the world really works, in modern slang
5 Hockey infraction
7 Target or J. C. Penney
8 Is wearing
9 Designer label letters

DOWN

1 Thought before blowing out the candles
2 Group of eight
3 Newsstand booth
4 Energy giant that went bankrupt in 2001
6 Millennials, informally

ACROSS

1 J. Edgar Hoover's org.
4 Ambulance wail
6 Man's name that's also something you'd find at a barbecue
7 Woman's name that's also something you'd find at a barbecue
8 Throws out of a contest, informally

DOWN

1 Toga party sites
2 Crooked
3 Black as night
4 Bay Area law enforcement org.
5 Saddam Hussein's land

52

1	2	3	4	5
6				
7				
8				
9				

ACROSS

1 Tortilla chip dip
6 Important bee
7 Reversed
8 Set things right
9 Amanda who starred in "She's the Man," 2006

DOWN

1 Young pigeon
2 Nickname for your uncle's wife
3 Gave false hopes
4 River that runs through Paris
5 World's longest mountain chain

53

¹N	²A	³V	⁴e	
⁵F	L	i	t	
⁶C	L	O	c	⁷K
	⁸A	L	O	e
	⁹H	A	N	g

ACROSS

1 Central part of a church
5 Movies, slangily
6 It has two hands, but no arms
8 ___ vera
9 Put up on the wall

DOWN

1 The Carolina Panthers play in it: Abbr.
2 God to more than a billion
3 Part of a string quartet
4 One just out of prison
7 Bar beer barrel

Allah

54

	1	2	3	4
5				
6				
7				
8				■

ACROSS

1 Musical finale
5 Handout to marathon runners
6 "I'll take a card," in blackjack
7 Creme-filled cookies
8 Poetic time of day

DOWN

1 Egypt's capital
2 Furry river animal
3 "Paranormal Activity" creature
4 Greek god of war
5 "To ___ it may concern"

ACROSS

1 Units of electrical resistance
5 Units of length
6 Channing of "21 Jump Street"
8 Sell
9 Units of work in physics

DOWN

1 Frequent, to a poet
2 "___-ho!" (cry when lifting)
3 Unit of length
4 Attacked by a jellyfish
7 Physicians: Abbr.

56

1	2	3	4	5
6				
7				
8				
9				

ACROSS

1 Utah landscape features
6 Fed-up person's cry
7 Drink slowly, as a beer
8 Presidential seal symbol
9 New parent's lack, often

DOWN

1 Where gold diggers can be found
2 Artificial sweetener in a blue packet
3 Increase in troop levels
4 Numbered supermarket area
5 Like a canyon's sides

	1	2	3	4
5				
6				
7				
8				

ACROSS

1 Gooey cheese
5 Yankee Stadium locale, with "the"
6 Diameter halves
7 Facebook creation
8 Piece next to a knight

DOWN

1 Channel for the Real Housewives franchise
2 Bull-riding contest
3 How contracts are usually signed
4 Glowing theater sign
5 ___ Rabbit

58

¹	²	³		
⁴			⁵	⁶
⁷				
⁸				
	⁹			

ACROSS

1 Buffoon
4 Anti-wrinkle treatment
7 Burst into flower
8 "Holy cow!"
9 Position for Pres. Obama, once

DOWN

1 Women's soccer star Wambach
2 Helpless?
3 Puts in the overhead compartment
5 Move like molasses
6 Marvel mutant superhero

1	2	3	4	■
5				■
6				7
■	8			
■	9			

ACROSS

1 Philosophical opposite of 1-Down
5 Modern-day Persia
6 2016 Australian Open champ Djokovic
8 Colt's mother
9 Friend in war

DOWN

1 Philosophical opposite of 1-Across
2 Enticing smell
3 The "N" of U.S.N.A.
4 Twist out of shape
7 Annoying item to lock in a car

60

ACROSS
1 Double-reed woodwind
5 **Like this clue**
6 Leap
7 Prefix with present or potent
8 Roe vs. ____

DOWN
1 President who appointed Kagan to the Supreme Court
2 Leap
3 Basic skateboarding trick
4 Summer hrs. in D.C.
6 Promise at a wedding

¹	²	³	⁴	⁵
⁶				
⁷				
⁸				
⁹				■

ACROSS

1 ___ Tuesday
6 Smiley face with hearts for eyes, e.g.
7 Cracker spreads
8 Admission of ineptitude
9 Helper: Abbr.

DOWN

1 Tinting option once available on Instagram
2 Amherst campus, briefly
3 White House VIP
4 Kick out
5 Global conquest board game

ACROSS

1 Part of MoMA
4 2016 award for DiCaprio
6 Google Maps offering
7 Nail polish remover brand
8 "We ___ the 99%"

DOWN

1 Sharper than 90 degrees
2 Give stars on Yelp, say
3 Fearsome dino
4 Killer whale
5 Like milk that's gone bad

1	2	3	4	5
6				
7				
8				
9				

ACROSS
1 Threw in
6 One in front of a train?
7 Medicine that helps alleviate hangovers
8 Artistic skill
9 Birthplace of Obama's father

DOWN
1 Taken ____ (stunned)
2 Rapper/producer with a professional title
3 Backless sofa
4 Spiritually enlighten
5 U.S. airline that's also a river feature

	1	2	3	4
5				
6				
7				
8				

ACROSS

1 Diddly-squat
5 A lot, in Mexico
6 Outer space creature
7 Most-played half of a
45 record
8 Job

DOWN

1 Child's first name?
2 Litmus paper reddeners
3 Pinchable part of the face
4 Hawaiian region known for
its coffee
5 Sail supporter on a ship

ACROSS

1 Like 2016, but not 2015
5 Biscuit often served with tea
6 "Whole ___ Love"
   (Led Zeppelin hit)
7 On the lookout
8 Extremely

DOWN

1 French place of learning
2 Super Tuesday participant
3 ___-level job
4 Without ice, as a drink
5 Czech or Serb

ACROSS

1 It may be put in a bun
5 T. rex and others
7 Card that tops all others
8 Italian scooter
9 Musical silence

DOWN

1 Sports bar wall hanging
2 Broadcaster
3 Occupied, as a lavatory
4 Easy victories
6 Went "ptui!"

ACROSS

1 ___ party
5 Prominent features of an Obama caricature
6 First-string players
8 Prefix meaning "half"
9 Sulky mood

DOWN

1 ___ Party
2 Hand-on-the-Bible utterances
3 ___ Party
4 "Me too!"
7 School that hosts an annual Mystery Hunt

68

ACROSS
1 ___ across (span)
4 Playful escapade (also a bird)
5 Soldier toy from Hasbro
6 [The clue for this answer is hidden elsewhere in this puzzle]
7 Chastising sound

DOWN
1 Pat of "Wheel of Fortune"
2 Waffle ___
3 Classic Jaguar model
4 They may be smacked, locked or sealed
5 Astronomer's std. at 0° longitude

1	2	3	4	5
6				
7				
8				
9				

ACROSS

1 "That's super cool"
6 "Toy Story" studio
7 Capital of Ghana
8 Chastise
9 Minister's home

DOWN

1 Kind of a jerk?
2 Pagan nature religion
3 Past prisoner, for short
4 Noblemen ranking above viscounts
5 What the Trans-Pacific Partnership deals with

70

	1	2	3	4
5				
6				
7				
8				

ACROSS

1 Fruit with a "check the neck" ripeness test
5 Disney character with big ears
6 New York City's ___ West Side
7 Spiteful, as gossip
8 A piano has 88

DOWN

1 Cocoon dwellers
2 Like some calories and promises
3 Assists with a crime
4 One of the Gilmore Girls
5 "Watch out for your head!"

ACROSS

1 Meat product sold in tins
5 With 5-Down, "Anyhoo . . ."
6 I.R.S. investigation
7 Store away for later
8 ___ of Capri

DOWN

1 Closes, as a door
2 Propel a swan boat, maybe
3 Spring up
4 Drug in "Breaking Bad"
5 See 5-Across

72

	1	2	3	4
5				
6				
7				
8				

ACROSS

1 Facebook button with "reactions"
5 Wooden frame for a painter
6 ___ Mountains, range from Morocco to Tunisia
7 This Greek letter: θ
8 Tennis match make-up

DOWN

1 Wood-shaping tool
2 Tiny bit of land in a lake
3 "Ode on a Grecian Urn" poet
4 Queen in Disney's "Frozen"
5 Chows down on

1	2	3	4	■
5				6
7				
8				
■	9			

ACROSS

1 _____ Strauss jeans
5 School founded by Ben Franklin, informally
7 Screenplay unit
8 Problems with old socks
9 Tasting like Granny Smith apples

DOWN

1 Growing luxuriantly, as plants
2 Disney theme park
3 Siren-like creature in the Harry Potter books
4 Word before tube or monologue
6 Destination for a return flight?

74

1	2	3	4	5
6				
7				
8				
9				

ACROSS

1 ___ Foods
6 DNA molecule's structure
7 Best of the best
8 Not even once
9 Nonreactive, chemically

DOWN

1 "___ Was Your Man" (2013 #1 hit for Bruno Mars)
2 Mirren of "The Queen"
3 Martini garnish
4 Soda bottle size
5 Apply, as pressure

ACROSS

1 Presidential ____
4 Democracy in action
5 Give more weapons to
6 Online market for handmade crafts
7 One calling the kettle black

DOWN

1 Talk a big game
2 "Lord knows ____!"
3 Blue, politically: Abbr.
4 Political anagram of 4-Across
5 Red, politically: Abbr.

ACROSS

1 With 4-Across, Indian tourist mecca
4 See 1-Across
6 10, in Italian
7 Boa or cobra
8 Fantasy football boons, for short

DOWN

1 Sully
2 In the lead
3 Deck foursome
4 They work in ERs
5 Nose lengthener for Pinocchio

	1	2	3	4
5				
6				
7				
8				

ACROSS

1 Give to one's Kickstarter, say
5 "And there you have it!"
6 "Cut ___" ("Stop that")
7 Big name in surround sound
8 The Earth turns on it

DOWN

1 Anti-wrinkle treatment
2 Garlicky sauce
3 ♣
4 Pop star Perry
5 "Livin' la ___ Loca"

ACROSS

1 ___ school
4 Picks up the check
5 Roadside inn
6 Hospital workers, informally
7 "Be quiet!"

DOWN

1 ___ Day, when students find out their postgraduate residency programs
2 Optometrists' interest
3 Internet connection that largely replaced dial-up
4 Winnie-the-___
5 Hospital workers, briefly

ACROSS

1 Elementary school math problems
5 It has cities named Bountiful, Paradise and Providence
6 Turn into a pulp
8 Iranian currency
9 Typical, with "the"

DOWN

1 "Yo, how's it goin'"
2 About-face in a car
3 "Super" video game character
4 Clip wool from
7 Dutch ___ disease

80

1	2	3	4	5
6				
7				
8				
9				

ACROSS

1 Org. co-founded by W.E.B. Du Bois
6 An ice place to live
7 Filling material for a tiler
8 Artichoke center
9 Shelters near a fire

DOWN

1 "See ya in the morning"
2 Be of the same mind
3 Take out ____ (borrow money)
4 Place for a suit case?
5 Mrs. ____ (porcelain character in "Beauty and the Beast")

ACROSS

1 Capturing maneuver in checkers
5 Steroids taker
6 Highly unconventional
7 Word after biological or atomic
8 French military cap

DOWN

1 Unit of energy
2 "Give me a high five!"
3 Parisian "Thanks"
4 President Obama advocated for this to be universal
5 Bottom row of icons on a Mac computer

ACROSS

1 Like a joke that refers to the fact that it's a joke
5 Swear
6 With 7-Across, trip on a jet
7 See 6-Across
8 Gave a thumbs-up

DOWN

1 Zayn _____, former One Direction heartthrob
2 Sidestep
3 Firm, as abs
4 Impress and then some
6 Opposite of con

ACROSS

1 "The Sopranos" group
4 Website with the Political Gabfest podcast
6 Everglades wader
7 Everglades wader
8 ___ latte (certain Starbucks order)

DOWN

1 Tie the knot
2 Great Plains tribe
3 Crooked
4 "___ out of your league, man"
5 Toy with its own theme park and movie

84

1	2	3	4	5
6				
7				
8				
9				

ACROSS

1 Goatees grow on them
6 "When the ___ Breaks" (Led Zeppelin song)
7 From another planet
8 They go down in the winter
9 Entourage

DOWN

1 Necklace fastener
2 "Wassup," more formally
3 Princeton, Dartmouth, Columbia, etc.
4 Food, shelter, and clothing
5 Fashion ___

ACROSS

1 Alternative to gov or edu
4 The "U" in E.U.
7 Geological feature that's also the name of a Montana city
8 Computer text code
9 Cable channel with a lot of sales pitches

DOWN

1 Historic 2016 Obama destination
2 Burden
3 McConnell of the Senate
5 R&B legend Redding
6 "No," to the Germans

ACROSS

1 Forensics show with several spinoffs
4 Parts of molecules
7 Italian port, or a type of salami
8 Poet Dickinson
9 These, in French

DOWN

1 Safety item when diving with great white sharks
2 Flower supporter
3 Kind of bond in chemistry
5 Unit in chemistry used to measure 4-Across
6 Utters

ACROSS

1 Cooking spray brand
4 HBO show about the record industry
6 Excuse in court
7 Wandering sort
8 ___ Radio Hour (popular N.P.R. podcast)

DOWN

1 Air Force employee
2 Japanese cartoon style
3 "Whoops, that one's on me"
4 Car for a large family
5 Blow the ___ off (expose)

ACROSS

1 "Mesquite" chip flavor
4 Louisiana wetland
6 Like some former government agents
7 Explosion
8 Suffix for musket, racket or puppet

DOWN

1 Overwhelmingly
2 Moves up and down on the waves
3 Leave one's job
4 New Mexican?
5 Connector of car wheels

ACROSS

1 Corner Monopoly square
5 Muslim holy city
6 Modify
7 Epic story divided into 24 books
8 Wildcat with tufted ears

DOWN

1 Peanut butter's partner
2 Be a part of, as a play
3 Tool used in alpine climbing
4 Animal fat
5 Iron clothes?

90

1	2	3	4	5
6				
7				
8				
9				

ACROSS

1 Habitat for bitterns and egrets
6 Thrill
7 "American Psycho" author Bret Easton ___
8 E-Z Pass stations
9 New York Times section

DOWN

1 TV's Boy ___ World
2 Divvy up
3 Presidential campaign event
4 "Yeah, but even so . . ."
5 Nobelist author of "Siddhartha"

	1	2	3	4
5				
6				
7				
8				

ACROSS

1 Zap with a stun gun
5 Quick kisses
6 Not cool
7 Snapchat feature
8 Whiskey serving

DOWN

1 Like "J" in the alphabet
2 Sound of a sneeze
3 Garment that also means "sidestep"
4 Award named after a TV network
5 ___ in Boots (Shrek character)

92

ACROSS

1 An A student has a high one, for short
4 Saudi Arabian currency
6 With 7-Across, annual prank exclamation
7 See 6-Across
8 N.F.L. scores

DOWN

1 Some urban food cart offerings
2 Aid for sand castle builders
3 "___ fair in love and war"
4 Transport for Huck and Jim
5 Device with earbuds

	1	2	3	4
5				
6				
7				
8				

ACROSS

1 Sierra ___ (soda)
5 Bird in the #BirdieSanders meme
6 MacDowell of "Groundhog Day"
7 Figure of speech
8 Speaker of the House Paul

DOWN

1 Actress/comedian Kaling
2 Country between Pakistan and Bangladesh
3 Offspring
4 Not us
5 Partner of square

94

	1	2	3	4
5				
6				
7				
8				

ACROSS

1 "Rubber" bath toy
5 Indian city that sounds like a good place to get a sandwich
6 The days of Hannukah, e.g.
7 Farm females
8 Miles and miles away

DOWN

1 Evening coffee choice
2 Prefix with sound and marathon
3 One might start "Two, four, six, eight, who do we appreciate!"
4 First-aid containers
5 Law prohibiting same-sex unions, familiarly

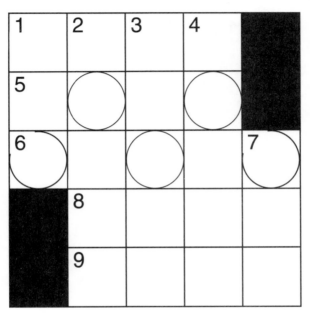

ACROSS

1 Spoiled kid
5 Like higher-ups in the Mafia
6 Old ___ tale
8 Function represented by the circled letters
9 "What ___ is new?"

DOWN

1 Audi rival
2 Proposed change of the minimum wage, e.g.
3 Popular pain reliever
4 Many users of Snapchat and Instagram
7 Get the picture

96

ACROSS

1 Word rhymed with "home" in "God Bless America"
5 Specialized vocab
6 Prefix for physics or turf
7 The T.S.A. makes you remove them
8 Variety

DOWN

1 Suspicious
2 ". . . with a cherry ___"
3 Think alike
4 Sounds from cows
5 John Oliver's "___ Week Tonight"

ACROSS

1 "The Bachelor" channel
4 Places to install solar panels
7 Santa ___ (famous ship)
8 House in "Game of Thrones"
9 Loser at the Battle of Gettysburg

DOWN

1 Gives weapons
2 Yacht or dinghy
3 Great Barrier Reef makeup
5 Matches produce them
6 "For Pete's ___!"

98

	1	2	3	4
5				
6				
7				
8				

ACROSS

1 App with a "Write a Review" function
5 Floyd Mayweather or Manny Pacquiao
6 "Straight ___ Compton"
7 "Rainbow" fish
8 "I could really use a hand here!"

DOWN

1 "___ one to talk!"
2 Shower with praise
3 Abate
4 Prefix with fall
5 This one and that one

S	P	U	R	S
P	O	P	U	P
L	O	T	S	A
A	C	H	E	D
T	H	E	S	E

ACROSS

1 N.B.A. Western Conference team
6 Annoying Internet ad
7 "___ luck!"
8 Felt soreness
9 "We hold ___ truths to be self-evident"

DOWN

1 Sound of a paintball on impact
2 Doggie
3 ___ ante (increase stakes)
4 Deceptive ploys
5 Garden tool

ACROSS

1 Adobe Acrobat files
5 _____ Garner, subject of police brutality protests
6 Watergate president
8 Unadulterated
9 Gush forth

DOWN

1 Something you can't complete the S.A.T. in
2 Plumbing problems
3 Mend
4 Bit of SportsCenter news
7 The "N" of N.Y.S.E.

	1	2	3	4
5				
6				
7				
8				

ACROSS

1 Enter a poker pot
5 BB-8 in "Star Wars," for one
6 Getting older
7 Out of practice
8 String of islands off Florida

DOWN

1 Squabble
2 What "obstreperous" and "clamorous" both mean
3 Shades of color
4 Pushing the envelope
5 Turkey meat choice

ACROSS

1 1+2+3, e.g.
4 ♠
6 Rotating point
7 Blue W for Microsoft Word and others
8 ___'easter

DOWN

1 Relish
2 Japanese soup noodles
3 2015 World Series team
4 Decide not to solve or buy a vowel
5 ___ de gallo (salsa)

ACROSS

1 Grp. involved in back-to-school night
4 Animals flying in a V formation
6 High-I.Q. crew
7 Like a day with blue skies
8 Really messy room, metaphorically

DOWN

1 Things in a compost bucket
2 Core principle
3 Rate for purity, as ore
4 Yukon S.U.V. maker
5 Site of the smallest bone in the human body

104

ACROSS

1 Include secretly on an email, for short
4 Harry Potter's mount
6 Certain Ivy Leaguer
7 N.C.A.A. women's basketball powerhouse
8 Stammering sounds

DOWN

1 "___ yourself" ("Get ready")
2 1997 addition to the front page of The New York Times
3 Nickel and dime
4 Utah sch. that Mitt Romney attended
5 Restroom sign

	1	2	3	4
5				
6				
7				
8				

ACROSS

1 Laundromat loss, perhaps
5 Russian city that hosted the 2014 Winter Olympics
6 Soccer shoe feature
7 Racetrack shapes
8 Six-mile-plus race, briefly

DOWN

1 Conquer, as a crossword
2 Swell place?
3 Hopscotch player's need
4 Baby foxes
5 Native of Glasgow

	1	2	3	4
5				
6				
7				
8				

ACROSS

1 Clock sound

5 2022 World Cup host embroiled in a corruption scandal

6 Taste that's not sweet, sour, bitter or salty

7 Top-notch

8 There are 14 in a fortnight

DOWN

1 Florida city on the Gulf Coast

2 Where Fiats are made

3 "The Stranger" novelist

4 Kardashian matriarch

5 Thigh muscle, informally

ACROSS

1 Video shooter, for short
4 Harlem ___ (dance craze of 2013)
6 Locale for much of The Da Vinci Code
7 Pizzeria fixtures
8 Annual conference with the slogan "Ideas worth spreading"

DOWN

1 Gave a hoot
2 Similar (to)
3 Extreme disarray
4 Protect, as a gym lifter
5 Possess

108

	1	2	3	4
5				
6				
7				
8				

ACROSS

1 Word in French restaurant names
5 Spanish for "fire"
6 Compadre
7 Nitro and Kingda Ka at Six Flags, for two
8 Oklahoma city

DOWN

1 Curry ingredient
2 "Project Runway" judge Klum
3 Provoked, with "on"
4 Where the wild things are?
5 New Yorker's MetroCard payment, e.g.

ACROSS

1 Airfare add-on
4 Amazon, to Barnes & Noble
6 Remove, as pencil marks
7 Alternative to U.P.S.
8 Singer Lana ___ Rey

DOWN

1 Given the ax
2 Dodge
3 Painter's stand
4 Official with a whistle
5 ___ Luthor of "Superman"

110

	1	2	3	4
	5			
6				
7				
8				

ACROSS

1 TV drama that began with a plane crash
5 On a single occasion
6 Line in Liverpool
7 Container for poison, maybe
8 It's silenced before a movie

DOWN

1 FX comedy that Jay Leno, Jerry Seinfeld and Amy Poehler have appeared on
2 N.B.A. great who stars in Icy Hot commercials
3 Regatta racer
4 Buttonless shirt
6 Home shopper's channel

ACROSS

1 Harry Potter's mark
5 "An Enquiry Concerning Human Understanding" philosopher
6 Intellectually unstimulating
7 Purple spring bloomer
8 Rx's

DOWN

1 Show to one's social media followers
2 Valentine's Day symbol
3 Not quite right
4 The "R" of Roy G. Biv
6 Energy

ACROSS
1 Take to court
4 With 3-Down, Emmy-winning role on "Orange is the New Black"
6 Protruding belly button
7 Sophomores or seniors
8 Documentary filmmaker Burns

DOWN
1 The devil
2 Submachine guns
3 See 4-Across
4 Hen's mate
5 "No shirt, no shoes, no service," e.g.

	1	2	3	4
5				
6				
7				
8				

ACROSS

1 Softly hit ball in tennis
5 Honda Accord or Toyota Camry
6 Speak one's mind
7 Something skipped on a lake
8 "Holy cow!"

DOWN

1 The third dimension
2 Challenge for a foreign language learner
3 Job for Mrs. Doubtfire or Mary Poppins
4 ___-slapper (funny joke)
5 Not bad, not good

	1	2	3	4
	5			
6				
7				
8				

ACROSS

1 Difficult journey
5 Bagel's center
6 Turkey topper
7 Downward dog or crescent moon
8 Movie lot constructions

DOWN

1 Painful sensation
2 Cook, as a turkey
3 North Pole workers
4 B sharp, for one
6 Feature of the Google Maps app

ACROSS

1 Lower, as the lights
4 Chess side that moves first
6 Therefore
7 Slices per pizza, often
8 Otis Redding's "___ A Little Tenderness"

DOWN

1 Dark and dreary
2 Poison ivy symptom
3 Date on a track team's schedule
4 Stimulate, as an appetite
5 One named in a will

116

	1	2	3	4
5				
6				
7				
8				

ACROSS

1 Accessory for Miss America
5 Food often served with ginger and wasabi
6 Is wearing
7 In the open
8 _____ Davidson, youngest cast member on "S.N.L."

DOWN

1 Charming and confident
2 Valued possession
3 Beach
4 "This answer is an anagram of THIN," for example
5 Black Friday sale offerer

1	2	3	4	5
6				
7				
8				
9				

ACROSS

1 Muscle twitch
6 Furry companion
7 Employee's angry cry
8 There's no such thing as a free one
9 Onionlike vegetables

DOWN

1 Something listed and endorsed on LinkedIn
2 Arouse, as interest
3 Carry ____ (sing on key)
4 Unit of butter
5 "Bulls hate the color red" and others

118

	1	2	3	4
	5			
6				
7				
8				

ACROSS

1 Crow's cries
5 Soul singer Redding
6 "___ feel my face" (comment on a freezing day)
7 Freezing
8 Bovines that live in freezing temperatures

DOWN

1 Wintertime drink
2 "We need to have ___"
3 Chilling things in winter storms
4 Fast jet, for short
6 Like winter sidewalks

ACROSS

1 They follow upsilons in the Greek alphabet
5 Unit of sugar or coal
6 Skittish
7 And others: Abbr.
8 "They're gr-r-reat!" tiger

DOWN

1 Demoted planet
2 Stay ____, house band for "The Late Show with Stephen Colbert"
3 Say without really saying
4 Cloak-and-dagger sort
6 Boeing 747, e.g.

	1	2	3	4
	5			
6				
7				■
8				■

ACROSS

1 Samsung Galaxy downloads
5 Computer partner of drop
6 Something seen before a Pixar film
7 Los Angeles Lakers legend
8 Chills in a champagne bucket

DOWN

1 Kind of committee
2 Exploratory spacecraft
3 Cuts the rind off
4 The Beatles' ___ Pepper
6 Bit of winter sports equipment

1	2	3		
4			5	6
7				
8				
		9		

ACROSS

1 Nothing
4 Wow
7 Had a meal
8 _____ 3000, one half of rap's OutKast
9 George W., vis-à-vis George H.W.

DOWN

1 Nothing
2 "Yeah, let's do it!"
3 Hits the tarmac
5 Nothing
6 Adam and Eve's garden

ACROSS

1 Affliction for returning soldiers, for short
5 The ___ State (Hawaii)
6 Main character on "Curb Your Enthusiasm"
7 First chips in the pot
8 Depict in a biased way

DOWN

1 Pirate ship feature
2 Rich cake
3 One "tamed" in a Shakespeare title
4 ___ Inn
5 "So it goes"

ACROSS

1 What software bugs are often found in
5 Drug rehab process, informally
6 Operation _____ Freedom (code name for a 2003 invasion)
7 Toyota hybrid
8 Post-Christmas store event

DOWN

1 Quotable Yogi
2 Shopping with virtual carts
3 Chef's hat
4 Graph line
5 Hummus and guacamole

124

	1	2	3
4	5		
6			
7			
8			

ACROSS

1 It comes with a charge
4 Spirit of Russia
6 David Foster Wallace piece
7 Kills it at a comedy club
8 Item in Santa's sack

DOWN

1 "If you ask me . . ."
2 Green-light
3 Anti votes
4 Crossing guard's wear
5 Capital of Norway

ACROSS

1 "It's just okay"
4 Site of 2015 British airstrikes
6 Tony, Oscar or Hugo
7 Some are noble
8 "Signs point to ___"
(Magic 8 Ball answer)

DOWN

1 Sinatra standard that begins "And now, the end is near"
2 Get rid of, as pencil marks
3 Adds to the payroll
4 Give in to gravity
5 What some people watch the Super Bowl for

ACROSS

1 SAT section
5 "Iliad" setting
6 Swore
8 Restaurant handout
9 Like 20% of Israel

DOWN

1 "Real World" network
2 Scent
3 Jeddah _____ (soon-to-be tallest building in the world)
4 "Laughing" animal
7 Confer knighthood on

ACROSS

1 Member of "New York's Finest"
4 Small egg
7 D.J.'s creation
8 "Hotline Bling" rapper, 2015
9 "Hang on a ___"

DOWN

1 Something "cut" by those dropping cable
2 ___ the top
3 Alternative to Nikes
5 Facebook button
6 Corp. higher-up

128

ACROSS

1 ___ de deux (dance for two)
4 Muslim garment that's banned in France
6 Office worker who'll help you after a crash
7 Comedian Anderson who hosted "Family Feud" from 1999–'02
8 Actor Beatty

DOWN

1 Stage, as a play
2 Squabble
3 Tentacled sea creature
4 "The Family Circus" cartoonist Keane
5 Sailor's yes

ACROSS

1 Buffoon
4 With 4-Down, much of the Southeast U.S. is in it
6 Part of the Sony hack
7 "12 Angry Men" director Sidney
8 Wand-waving group, for short

DOWN

1 "Hope" politician
2 "That's ___ and you know it!"
3 Pool table material
4 See 4-Across
5 Radio host Don

130

	1	2	3	
4				5
6				
7				
	8			

ACROSS

1 Dove's call
4 Father, informally
6 Citizenship seeker
7 With 5- and 1-Down, 2015 Album of the Year nominee by Alabama Shakes
8 Apt. units

DOWN

1 See 7-Across
2 Drug at the center of Great Britain/China wars
3 Unwraps
4 Faux ____
5 See 7-Across

¹	²	³	■	■
⁴			⁵	⁶
⁷				
⁸				
■	⁹			

ACROSS

1 ___ choy (Chinese vegetable)
4 "Hasta la vista!"
7 Thin and graceful
8 What follows going cold turkey
9 Where a telescope is aimed

DOWN

1 Like The Rock and Michael Jordan
2 Dog that's messed with by Garfield
3 Saint ___ and Nevis
5 "Gotcha"
6 Hot

132

<table>
<tr><td>1</td><td>2</td><td>3</td><td>4</td><td></td></tr>
<tr><td>5</td><td></td><td></td><td></td><td>6</td></tr>
<tr><td>7</td><td></td><td></td><td></td><td></td></tr>
<tr><td>8</td><td></td><td></td><td></td><td></td></tr>
<tr><td></td><td>9</td><td></td><td></td><td></td></tr>
</table>

ACROSS

1 Soothing ointment
5 Dodge
7 Dutch cheese with a yellow rind
8 Cheese named for its country of origin
9 Rogen of "The Night Before"

DOWN

1 Subject of airport inspections
2 Declares
3 Huey and Dewey's brother, in cartoons
4 In the ___ of (during)
6 Recipe sprinkling

ACROSS

1 Sign on an elementary school bathroom door
5 Prize won by Obama, Roosevelt and Carter
6 Oracle _____ (home of the Golden State Warriors)
7 Piquant
8 "You have no _____!"

DOWN

1 Like yawning students, say
2 Seriously chubby
3 Gossipy type
4 Kill, as a dragon
5 "Schindler's List" villain

ACROSS

1 ___ Emanuel, mayor of Chicago
5 Criminal's creation
7 "Now I understand!"
8 French river that's an anagram of MEMOS
9 Suffix with Oktober

DOWN

1 Opposite of riches, in a phrase
2 Standoffish
3 Words to a blackjack dealer
4 Injures badly
6 "Leave in," to a proofreader

1	2	3	4	5
6				
7				
8				
9				

ACROSS

1 Razzle-dazzle
6 Cheesy chip
7 Enjoyed a home-cooked meal
8 Beef cut that's also the name of a bad golf shot
9 Spells the wrong way?

DOWN

1 Grind together, as teeth
2 Wood-shaping tool
3 Climbing tool for frozen surfaces
4 "To ___ own self be true"
5 Passes (out)

136

	1	2	3	4
	5			
6				
7				
8				

ACROSS

1 With 8-Across, franchise with a noted 12/18/15 release

5 Holding your breath or gargling with ice water, for the hiccups

6 Wifey's partner

7 Follow orders

8 See 1-Across

DOWN

1 Explore a coral reef

2 Rutabaga or potato

3 Fast food chain known for its roast beef

4 Singer Lana Del ___

6 Incredulous question after a magic trick

ACROSS

1 It has an eye on the TV
4 U.C.L.A. athlete
6 Back in style
7 Flower that blooms in the fall
8 Highest tile value in Scrabble

DOWN

1 Family emblem
2 Isolated hill
3 Mythical creature in the Starbucks logo
4 Word with sports or training
5 Neither's partner

138

1	2	3	4	■
5				■
6				7
■	8			
■	9			

ACROSS

1 Gumbo veggie
5 Lifeguard's workplace
6 "Three things cannot long be hidden: the sun, the moon and the ___": Buddha
8 On an ocean voyage
9 Many a character on "The Big Bang Theory"

DOWN

1 Pick, with "for"
2 Book that begins "In the name of Allah . . ."
3 Awaken
4 Modify, as clothes
7 Possessed

ACROSS

1 Baseball slugger's stat
4 Homophone of 1-Down
5 Genre for do-it-yourself books
6 Poems of praise
7 Cruz in the 2016 election

DOWN

1 Manned the oars
2 Upside-down sleepers
3 When repeated, child's response to "Who wants more ice cream?"
4 Homophone of 1-Down
5 Like jalapeños

140

¹	²	³	■	■
⁴			⁵	⁶
⁷				
⁸				
■	■	⁹		

ACROSS

1 Feature of an HDTV screen
4 Trojan War epic
7 Minister's residence
8 Service from AOL or Microsoft Outlook
9 Japanese "yes"

DOWN

1 Fruit squeezed over pad thai
2 Chowder ingredient
3 "Someone's in the kitchen with ___" (line from "I've Been Working on the Railroad")
5 Turkey's place, for the most part
6 Turkey's place

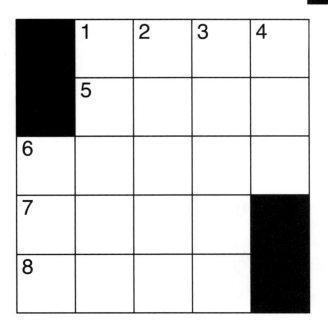

ACROSS
1 One way up a ski mountain
5 Inactive
6 "That is to say . . ."
7 One way up a ski mountain
8 Something found underfoot?

DOWN
1 Try to pass the bar?
2 Perfect
3 Broken-down motorist's signal
4 V : five :: X : ____
6 "____ all good"

142

¹	²	³	⁴	■
⁵				■
⁶				⁷
■	⁸			
■	⁹			

ACROSS

1 Slime
5 Movie-rating org.
6 "___ Christmas!"
8 Pixar fish
9 Actress Cannon of "Heaven Can Wait"

DOWN

1 "Delicious!"
2 Flip over
3 "All I Want for Christmas Is You" singer Mariah
4 Cosmic payback
7 Over there, quaintly

143

1	2	3	4	█
5				█
6				7
█	8			
█	9			

ACROSS

1 Midnight ____ (Christmas Eve service)
5 Prime draft status
6 First year of Obama's presidency, slangily
8 Abbr. on a historic building
9 Dec. 25

DOWN

1 Stock quote?
2 Building add-on
3 Earthquake
4 Traveler on Christmas Eve
7 Actors Burns and Asner

ACROSS

1 Piglet's mother
4 Roald Dahl's chocolatier
6 Blue ribbon or gold medal
7 "What happens here, stays here" sloganeer
8 Football field units: Abbr.

DOWN

1 Unexpected problems
2 Creole cooking vegetable
3 Fistfuls of money
4 Like permed hair
5 Was outstanding with money?

ACROSS

1 Forest ranger's worry
5 Lacking a knack for
6 Bit of hijinks
7 Secret supply
8 Herb often used in turkey stuffing

DOWN

1 Classic orange soda
2 Luggage attachment
3 Good worker's reward
4 Make quite an impression?
5 Prominent part of dubstep music

ACROSS

1 ___ deserts
5 Not deceived by
6 1979 film with the tagline "In space, no one can hear you scream"
7 Hummus scooper-upper
8 Sneak a look

DOWN

1 "Maleficent" star, 2014
2 Join forces
3 It might be ordered medium-rare
4 Truck scale unit
6 Snapchat or WeChat

ACROSS

1 Word after second, wild or educated
6 Open, as a toothpaste tube
7 Cognizant (of)
8 Brink
9 Value-___tax

DOWN

1 Tropical fruit
2 Not married
3 Hallmark.com offering
4 Beetle Bailey's boss
5 What people do when they're over 65?

148

	1	2	3	
4				5
6				
7				
	8			

ACROSS

1 With 4-Across, time for a big party
4 See 1-Across
6 When the Boston Marathon is run
7 Alternative to hoppy, as with beer
8 Corrosive substance

DOWN

1 Country with Mount Everest on its border
2 Ahead of schedule
3 Put pen to paper
4 Thanksgiving side dish vegetable
5 Sneaky

ACROSS

1 Gear tooth
4 "Yup"
7 Set of keys?
8 Drive-in fast-food chain
9 "Go ___ your mother"

DOWN

1 Coffeehouse containers
2 One of Pittsburgh's three rivers
3 West African nation
5 Les États-___
6 Sell at a pawnshop

150

ACROSS

1 Joe Biden represented it: Abbr.
4 Battle of the ___
6 "In memoriam" news items, briefly
7 Battle of the ___
8 Prefix with political or thermal

DOWN

1 Fix, as a computer program
2 What Edward Snowden is currently in
3 Fire from a job
4 Loudly weep
5 Opposite of NNW

ANSWERS

1

B	R	A	Y	■
Z	E	R	O	■
Z	A	I	U	S
■	P	E	R	U
■	S	L	E	D

2

■	S	L	I	P
C	H	I	N	O
L	I	M	B	O
I	F	E	E	L
P	T	S	D	■

3

■	S	T	A	R
■	H	U	G	O
L	I	L	A	C
I	R	I	S	■
D	E	P	P	■

4

E	Y	E		
R	E	L	A	X
A	L	B	U	M
S	P	O	R	E
		W	A	N

5

		H	I	P
C	R	E	D	O
H	U	M	O	R
A	D	E	L	E
R	E	N		

6

C	S	P	A	N
A	C	U	R	A
W	A	N	D	S
E	L	I	O	T
D	E	C	R	Y

7

A	R	M	S	
B	A	I	L	
S	T	A	I	R
	E	M	M	A
	D	I	E	T

8

	S	A	L	T
	T	R	U	E
C	R	I	M	E
H	A	S	P	
E	W	E	S	

9

W	I	L	D	
A	S	I	A	
Y	A	N	K	S
	A	D	A	Y
	C	A	R	D

10

		A	T	E
D	I	D	I	T
O	B	A	M	A
J	A	M	E	S
O	R	S		

11

		A	S	P
L	O	R	N	E
E	G	G	O	N
F	R	O	W	N
T	E	N		

12

		S	A	T
S	C	A	R	E
W	A	L	L	E
A	R	S	O	N
N	S	A		

13

A	C	T	S	
H	O	O	C	H
E	R	N	I	E
M	A	Y	O	R
	L	A	N	E

14

	S	A	F	E
D	A	V	I	D
A	M	O	N	G
B	O	W	I	E
S	A	S	S	

15

	F	L	Y	
P	L	A	I	D
C	O	D	E	R
T	A	L	L	Y
	T	E	D	

16

S	L	A	C	K
C	A	B	I	N
A	T	O	N	E
P	E	A	C	E
E	X	T	O	L

17

	S	A	N	S
M	O	G	U	L
A	N	I	T	A
R	A	T	T	Y
X	R	A	Y	

18

	C	A	R	P
L	O	N	E	R
A	L	G	A	E
M	O	L	L	Y
P	R	O	M	

19

	S	K	I	M
C	H	O	R	E
A	A	R	O	N
T	R	E	N	D
O	K	A	Y	

20

	S	E	A	
A	W	M	A	N
C	H	E	S	T
H	O	L	E	S
E	A	T		

21

D	R	Y		
R	I	O	T	S
A	C	U	R	A
G	E	T	U	P
		H	E	S

22

	J	A	Z	Z
T	A	B	O	O
A	M	I	N	O
R	I	D	E	S
S	E	E	D	

23

	C	A	L	
T	O	T	A	L
B	O	R	N	E
S	P	I	K	E
	S	A	Y	

24

G	I	G	S	
A	N	E	W	
S	I	N	E	W
	N	O	A	H
	K	A	T	Y

A	F	L	A	C
B	R	A	V	O
H	O	N	O	R
O	Z	Z	I	E
R	E	A	D	S

	A	M	S	
F	L	A	K	E
A	P	R	O	N
S	H	O	R	T
	A	N	T	

	A	W	A	Y
	G	A	M	E
J	O	N	A	S
A	N	T	Z	
N	Y	S	E	

28

	C	A	M
P	H	O	T	O
S	A	L	A	D
S	L	I	D	E
T	O	N		

29

	L	A	P	S
	O	R	A	L
H	O	R	N	Y
U	F	O	S	
H	A	Z	Y	

30

	S	E	C	
A	T	L	A	S
B	R	I	C	K
C	A	T	H	Y
	W	E	E	

31

	B	Y	T	E
C	R	E	A	M
R	E	A	L	M
E	A	R	L	Y
D	K	N	Y	

32

	M	V	P	S
	O	I	L	S
E	X	X	O	N
L	I	E	D	
M	E	N	S	

33

J	U	S		
U	P	E	N	N
N	O	W	A	Y
G	N	O	M	E
		N	E	T

34

		S	A	M
C	L	A	R	A
H	I	D	E	S
E	F	L	A	T
F	E	Y		

35

P	A	G	E	R
E	L	U	D	E
R	E	I	G	N
T	V	S	E	T
H	E	E	D	S

36

		T	I	E
B	R	O	N	X
L	A	T	K	E
O	K	A	Y	S
G	E	L		

37

A	S	H		
L	O	O	P	S
A	C	H	O	O
S	K	U	L	L
		M	O	O

38

	B	U	T	T
H	A	N	O	I
O	S	C	A	R
W	I	L	D	E
I	C	E	S	

39

C	O	D	E	S
O	C	E	A	N
N	H		G	A
C	O	W	E	R
H	A	V	R	E

40

	W	H	I	Z
	H	Y	D	E
T	I	E	I	N
A	N	N	O	
B	E	A	T	

41

	M	A	S	S
	O	B	I	E
S	T	A	K	E
I	T	C	H	
A	S	K	S	

42

	C	A	B	
A	D	L	I	B
P	I	A	N	O
E	M	P	T	Y
X	E	S		

C	H	A	W	
H	O	U	R	S
I	N	D	I	A
N	O	I	S	Y
	R	O	T	S

44

	S	T	A	T
	P	A	W	N
R	O	B	O	T
R	O	O	K	
S	L	O	E	

45

F	A	C	T	S
O	N	I	O	N
I	G	L	O	O
S	L	I	N	K
T	E	A	S	E

46

	S	A	K	E
P	A	G	A	N
A	M	E	N	D
T	O	N	Y	S
H	A	T	E	

47

	T	A	S	
M	A	R	C	O
R	U	B	I	O
S	P	O	O	F
	E	R	N	

48

A	C	M	E	
P	R	O	X	Y
P	A	S	T	A
S	P	U	R	N
	S	L	A	G

49

	T	O	A	D
H	O	N	D	A
I	D	E	A	L
G	A	U	G	E
H	Y	P	E	

50

W	O	K	E	
I	C	I	N	G
S	T	O	R	E
H	A	S	O	N
	D	K	N	Y

51

		F	B	I
S	I	R	E	N
F	R	A	N	K
P	A	T	T	Y
D	Q	S		

52

S	A	L	S	A
Q	U	E	E	N
U	N	D	I	D
A	T	O	N	E
B	Y	N	E	S

53

N	A	V	E	■
F	L	I	X	■
C	L	O	C	K
■	A	L	O	E
■	H	A	N	G

54

■	C	O	D	A
W	A	T	E	R
H	I	T	M	E
O	R	E	O	S
M	O	R	N	■

55

O	H	M	S	
F	E	E	T	
T	A	T	U	M
	V	E	N	D
	E	R	G	S

56

M	E	S	A	S
I	Q	U	I	T
N	U	R	S	E
E	A	G	L	E
S	L	E	E	P

57

	B	R	I	E
B	R	O	N	X
R	A	D	I	I
E	V	E	N	T
R	O	O	K	

58

A	S	S		
B	O	T	O	X
B	L	O	O	M
Y	O	W	Z	A
		S	E	N

59

Y	A	N	G	
I	R	A	N	
N	O	V	A	K
	M	A	R	E
	A	L	L	Y

60

	O	B	O	E
	B	O	L	D
V	A	U	L	T
O	M	N	I	
W	A	D	E	

61

S	U	P	E	R
E	M	O	J	I
P	A	T	E	S
I	S	U	C	K
A	S	S	T	■

62

■		A	R	T
O	S	C	A	R
R	O	U	T	E
C	U	T	E	X
A	R	E	■	

63

A	D	D	E	D
B	R	I	D	E
A	D	V	I	L
C	R	A	F	T
K	E	N	Y	A

64

	J	A	C	K
M	U	C	H	O
A	L	I	E	N
S	I	D	E	A
T	A	S	K	

65

	E	V	E	N
S	C	O	N	E
L	O	T	T	A
A	L	E	R	T
V	E	R	Y	

66

H	A	I	R	
D	I	N	O	S
T	R	U	M	P
V	E	S	P	A
	R	E	S	T

67

T	O	G	A	
E	A	R	S	
A	T	E	A	M
	H	E	M	I
	S	N	I	T

68

	S	I	X
	L	A	R	K
G	I	J	O	E
S	P	A	N	
T	S	K		

69

S	W	E	E	T
P	I	X	A	R
A	C	C	R	A
S	C	O	L	D
M	A	N	S	E

70

	P	E	A	R
D	U	M	B	O
U	P	P	E	R
C	A	T	T	Y
K	E	Y	S	

71

	S	P	A	M
W	H	E	R	E
A	U	D	I	T
S	T	A	S	H
I	S	L	E	

72

	L	I	K	E
E	A	S	E	L
A	T	L	A	S
T	H	E	T	A
S	E	T	S	

73

L	E	V	I	■
U	P	E	N	N
S	C	E	N	E
H	O	L	E	S
■	T	A	R	T

74

W	H	O	L	E
H	E	L	I	X
E	L	I	T	E
N	E	V	E	R
I	N	E	R	T

75

■	■	B	I	D
■	V	O	T	E
R	E	A	R	M
E	T	S	Y	■
P	O	T	■	■

76

	T	A	J	
M	A	H	A	L
D	I	E	C	I
S	N	A	K	E
	T	D	S	

77

	B	A	C	K
V	O	I	L	A
I	T	O	U	T
D	O	L	B	Y
A	X	I	S	

78

		M	E	D
	P	A	Y	S
M	O	T	E	L
D	O	C	S	
S	H	H		

79

S	U	M	S	
U	T	A	H	
P	U	R	E	E
	R	I	A	L
	N	O	R	M

80

N	A	A	C	P
I	G	L	O	O
G	R	O	U	T
H	E	A	R	T
T	E	N	T	S

81

	J	U	M	P
D	O	P	E	R
O	U	T	R	E
C	L	O	C	K
K	E	P	I	

82

	M	E	T	A
	A	V	O	W
P	L	A	N	E
R	I	D	E	
O	K	E	D	

83

		M	O	B
S	L	A	T	E
H	E	R	O	N
E	G	R	E	T
S	O	Y		

84

C	H	I	N	S
L	E	V	E	E
A	L	I	E	N
S	L	E	D	S
P	O	S	S	E

85

C	O	M		
U	N	I	O	N
B	U	T	T	E
A	S	C	I	I
		H	S	N

86

C	S	I		
A	T	O	M	S
G	E	N	O	A
E	M	I	L	Y
		C	E	S

87

	P	A	M	
V	I	N	Y	L
A	L	I	B	I
N	O	M	A	D
	T	E	D	

88

	B	B	Q
B	A	Y	O	U
E	X	F	B	I
B	L	A	S	T
E	E	R		

89

	J	A	I	L
M	E	C	C	A
A	L	T	E	R
I	L	I	A	D
L	Y	N	X	

90

M	A	R	S	H
E	L	A	T	E
E	L	L	I	S
T	O	L	L	S
S	T	Y	L	E

91

	T	A	S	E
P	E	C	K	S
U	N	H	I	P
S	T	O	R	Y
S	H	O	T	

92

	G	P	A
R	I	Y	A	L
A	P	R	I	L
F	O	O	L	S
T	D	S	

93

	M	I	S	T
F	I	N	C	H
A	N	D	I	E
I	D	I	O	M
R	Y	A	N	

94

	D	U	C	K
D	E	L	H	I
O	C	T	E	T
M	A	R	E	S
A	F	A	R	

95

B	R	A	T	
M	A	D	E	
W	I	V	E	S
	S	I	N	E
	E	L	S	E

96

	F	O	A	M
L	I	N	G	O
A	S	T	R	O
S	H	O	E	S
T	Y	P	E	

A	B	C		
R	O	O	F	S
M	A	R	I	A
S	T	A	R	K
		L	E	E

	Y	E	L	P
B	O	X	E	R
O	U	T	T	A
T	R	O	U	T
H	E	L	P	

S	P	U	R	S
P	O	P	U	P
L	O	T	S	A
A	C	H	E	D
T	H	E	S	E

100

P	D	F	S	
E	R	I	C	
N	I	X	O	N
	P	U	R	E
	S	P	E	W

101

	A	N	T	E
D	R	O	I	D
A	G	I	N	G
R	U	S	T	Y
K	E	Y	S	

102

		S	U	M
S	P	A	D	E
P	I	V	O	T
I	C	O	N	S
N	O	R		

103

	P	T	A	
G	E	E	S	E
M	E	N	S	A
C	L	E	A	R
	S	T	Y	

104

	B	C	C	
B	R	O	O	M
Y	A	L	I	E
U	C	O	N	N
	E	R	S	

105

	S	O	C	K
S	O	C	H	I
C	L	E	A	T
O	V	A	L	S
T	E	N	K	

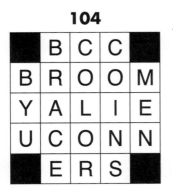

106

	T	I	C	K
Q	A	T	A	R
U	M	A	M	I
A	P	L	U	S
D	A	Y	S	

107

		C	A	M
S	H	A	K	E
P	A	R	I	S
O	V	E	N	S
T	E	D		

108

	C	H	E	Z
F	U	E	G	O
A	M	I	G	O
R	I	D	E	S
E	N	I	D	

109

	F	E	E	
R	I	V	A	L
E	R	A	S	E
F	E	D	E	X
	D	E	L	

110

	L	O	S	T
	O	N	C	E
Q	U	E	U	E
V	I	A	L	
C	E	L	L	

111

	S	C	A	R
	H	U	M	E
V	A	P	I	D
I	R	I	S	
M	E	D	S	

	S	U	E	
C	R	A	Z	Y
O	U	T	I	E
C	L	A	S	S
K	E	N		

	D	I	N	K
S	E	D	A	N
O	P	I	N	E
S	T	O	N	E
O	H	M	Y	

	T	R	E	K
	H	O	L	E
G	R	A	V	Y
P	O	S	E	
S	E	T	S	

		D	I	M
W	H	I	T	E
H	E	N	C	E
E	I	G	H	T
T	R	Y		

116

	S	A	S	H
S	U	S	H	I
H	A	S	O	N
O	V	E	R	T
P	E	T	E	

117

S	P	A	S	M
K	I	T	T	Y
I	Q	U	I	T
L	U	N	C	H
L	E	E	K	S

118

	C	A	W	S
	O	T	I	S
I	C	A	N	T
C	O	L	D	
Y	A	K	S	

119

	P	H	I	S
	L	U	M	P
J	U	M	P	Y
E	T	A	L	
T	O	N	Y	

120

	A	P	P	S
	D	R	A	G
S	H	O	R	T
K	O	B	E	
I	C	E	S	

121

N	I	L		
A	M	A	Z	E
D	I	N	E	D
A	N	D	R	E
		S	O	N

122

	P	T	S	D
A	L	O	H	A
L	A	R	R	Y
A	N	T	E	S
S	K	E	W	

123

	B	E	T	A
D	E	T	O	X
I	R	A	Q	I
P	R	I	U	S
S	A	L	E	

124

	I	O	N
V	O	D	K	A
E	S	S	A	Y
S	L	A	Y	S
T	O	Y		

125

	M	E	H	
S	Y	R	I	A
A	W	A	R	D
G	A	S	E	S
	Y	E	S	

126

M	A	T	H	
T	R	O	Y	
V	O	W	E	D
	M	E	N	U
	A	R	A	B

C	O	P		
O	V	U	L	E
R	E	M	I	X
D	R	A	K	E
		S	E	C

	P	A	S	
B	U	R	Q	A
I	T	G	U	Y
L	O	U	I	E
	N	E	D	

		O	A	F
B	I	B	L	E
E	M	A	I	L
L	U	M	E	T
T	S	A		

130

	C	O	O	
P	O	P	P	A
A	L	I	E	N
S	O	U	N	D
	R	M	S	

131

B	O	K		
A	D	I	O	S
L	I	T	H	E
D	E	T	O	X
		S	K	Y

132

B	A	L	M	
A	V	O	I	D
G	O	U	D	A
S	W	I	S	S
	S	E	T	H

133

	B	O	Y	S
N	O	B	E	L
A	R	E	N	A
Z	E	S	T	Y
I	D	E	A	

134

R	A	H	M	
A	L	I	A	S
G	O	T	I	T
S	O	M	M	E
	F	E	S	T

135

G	L	I	T	Z
N	A	C	H	O
A	T	E	I	N
S	H	A	N	K
H	E	X	E	S

136

	S	T	A	R	
	C	U	R	E	
H	U	B	B	Y	
O	B	E	Y		
W	A	R	S		

137

	C	B	S	
B	R	U	I	N
R	E	T	R	O
A	S	T	E	R
	T	E	N	

138

O	K	R	A	
P	O	O	L	
T	R	U	T	H
	A	S	E	A
	N	E	R	D

139

			R	B	I
		R	O	A	D
	H	O	W	T	O
	O	D	E	S	
	T	E	D		

140

L	C	D		
I	L	I	A	D
M	A	N	S	E
E	M	A	I	L
		H	A	I

141

	L	I	F	T
	I	D	L	E
I	M	E	A	N
T	B	A	R	
S	O	L	E	

142

M	U	C	K	
M	P	A	A	
M	E	R	R	Y
	N	E	M	O
	D	Y	A	N

143

M	A	S	S	
O	N	E	A	
O	N	I	N	E
	E	S	T	D
	X	M	A	S

144

		S	O	W
W	O	N	K	A
A	W	A	R	D
V	E	G	A	S
Y	D	S		

145

	F	I	R	E
B	A	D	A	T
A	N	T	I	C
S	T	A	S	H
S	A	G	E	

146

	J	U	S	T
	O	N	T	O
A	L	I	E	N
P	I	T	A	
P	E	E	K	

147

G	U	E	S	S
U	N	C	A	P
A	W	A	R	E
V	E	R	G	E
A	D	D	E	D

148

	N	E	W	
Y	E	A	R	S
A	P	R	I	L
M	A	L	T	Y
	L	Y	E	

149

C	O	G		
U	H	H	U	H
P	I	A	N	O
S	O	N	I	C
		A	S	K

150

	D	E	L	
S	E	X	E	S
O	B	I	T	S
B	U	L	G	E
	G	E	O	

Looking for more Hard Crosswords?

The New York Times

The #1 Name in Crosswords

Looking for more Large-Print Crosswords?

The New York Times

The #1 Name in Crosswords

Looking for more Sunday Crosswords?

The New York Times

The #1 Name in Crosswords

once
a·day

25

DAYS OF ADVENT

NIV

once
a·day

25

DAYS OF ADVENT

Kenneth Boa
with
John Allen Turner

ZONDERVAN®

ZONDERVAN

Once-A-Day 25 Days of Advent Devotional
Copyright © 2012 by Kenneth Boa

This title is also available as a Zondervan ebook.
Visit www.zondervan.com/ebooks.

All rights reserved.

Requests for information should be addressed to:

Zondervan, *Grand Rapids, Michigan 49530*

Library of Congress Cataloging-in-Publication Data

Boa, Kenneth.
    Once-a-day, 25 days of Advent devotional / written by Ken Boa.
      p. cm. – (Once-a-day)
    ISBN 978-0-310-41913-6 (booklet)
  1. Advent – Prayers and devotions. I. Title. II. Title: Once-a-day,
twenty-five days of Advent devotional.
    BV40.B58 2012
    242'.332 – dc23   2012018156

Any Internet addresses (websites, blogs, etc.) and telephone numbers in this book are offered as a resource. They are not intended
in any way to be or imply an endorsement by Zondervan, nor does
Zondervan vouch for the content of these sites and numbers for
the life of this book.

Cover design: Faceout Studio and Jamie DeBruyn
Interior design: Sherri Hoffman and Jamie DeBruyn

Printed in the United States of America

12 13 14 15 16 /OPP/ 16 15 14 13 12 11 10 9 8 7 6 5 4 3 2 1

CONTENTS

PREFACE

Advent and the Mystery of the Incarnation

All praise to Thee, Eternal Lord
Clothed in a garb of flesh and blood;
Choosing a manger for a throne,
While worlds on worlds are Thine alone.

Martin Luther

Although we live in a pluralistic culture that tells us that Christianity is just one option in a whole cafeteria of equally valid spiritual choices, a closer look at the Bible reveals its profound uniqueness. Its claims about God, humanity and the way of salvation set it apart from other religions, and this uniqueness is especially evident in the person and work of the Lord Jesus Christ. Who could have imagined that the transcendent Creator of the universe would have personally visited our planet, even in splendor and majesty? But the Gospels go far beyond this: They reveal that the King of Creation came in the weakness and vulnerability of a little child—a child who would grow up to be spurned and rejected by his own people—a man of sorrows whose suffering and death would purchase the gift of divine forgiveness and eternal life.

As the decisive revelation of the transcendent God in human history, the incarnation is the central mystery of the Christian faith. Through it, the eternal Word took on human flesh and experienced the limitations, sorrows, joys and temptations of humanness, yet was without sin or imperfection.

My friend John Alan Turner has crafted a wonderful series of reflections that will guide you through this Advent season to prepare you for your celebration of the mystery of the incarnation. Each of the 25 days has a series of Scriptures, a meditation and a prayer that will enrich and elevate your thoughts as you reflect on the Biblical meaning of Christmas and its relevance for your life today.

Kenneth Boa, April 2012

day 1

GENESIS 1:1,26–28,31

In the beginning God created the heavens and the earth. Then God said, "Let us make mankind in our image, in our likeness, so that they may rule over the fish in the sea and the birds in the sky, over the livestock and all the wild animals, and over all the creatures that move along the ground." So God created mankind in his own image, in the image of God he created them; male and female he created them. God blessed them and said to them, "Be fruitful and increase in number; fill the earth and subdue it. Rule over the fish in the sea and the birds in the sky and over every living creature that moves on the ground." God saw all that he had made, and it was very good. And there was evening, and there was morning—the sixth day.

JOHN 1:1–5

In the beginning was the Word, and the Word was with God, and the Word was God. He was with God in the beginning. Through him all things were made; without him nothing was made that has been made. In him was life, and that life was the light of all mankind. The light shines in the darkness, and the darkness has not overcome it.

EPHESIANS 2:10

For we are God's handiwork, created in Christ Jesus to do good works, which God prepared in advance for us to do.

MEDITATION

As we begin this Advent season, we look forward to Christmas, to the celebration of the birth of Christ. The whole world seems to be focused only on the baby. But this is no ordinary baby. As difficult as this may be to understand, let us not forget that this baby was present from the beginning, long before his birth on this earth. Nothing was created without him, not anything in the heavens above, not anything on the earth below, and certainly not us. "Then God said, 'Let us make mankind in *our* image, in *our* likeness'" (Genesis 1:26, emphasis added).

The secrets of time and space and eternity are found in this One, the Son of God, our Creator, our Sustainer, the One whose image we bear. It is only in him that we find our true dignity and purpose as people. He is the author and finisher of our faith, the One who remains faithful even when we are faithless. His entrance into our world means that we too can become all that God intended for us when he created us, that we may become more and more like his Son, who is "the radiance of God's glory and the exact representation of his being" (Hebrews 1:3).

PRAYER

Thank you, sovereign Lord and Creator, for this day of be-
ginnings and remembering. Thank you for making us in your
glorious image, for honoring us with dignity and purpose.
We praise you in this season of remembering who you truly
are and how you have drawn near to us because of your
great love for us. Give us wisdom as we prepare to cele-
brate the birth of the Son you sent to us. We will rejoice in
this season of remembering, knowing that everything you
have ever given and done is always not simply good but
very good. It is in Jesus' name we pray. Amen. ♣

day2

GENESIS 3:4–5,7–8,14–15,22–23

"You will not certainly die," the serpent said to the woman. "For God knows that when you eat from [the tree] your eyes will be opened, and you will be like God, knowing good and evil."

Then the eyes of both [the woman and her husband] were opened, and they realized they were naked … and they hid from the LORD God among the trees of the garden.

So the LORD God said to the serpent, "Because you have done this … I will put enmity between you and the woman, and between your offspring and hers; he will crush your head, and you will strike his heel."

And the LORD God said, "The man has now become like one of us, knowing good and evil" … So the LORD God banished him from the Garden of Eden.

ISAIAH 59:1–2

Surely the arm of the LORD is not too short to save, nor his ear too dull to hear. But your iniquities have separated you from your God; your sins have hidden his face from you, so that he will not hear.

ROMANS 5:12–19

Therefore, just as sin entered the world through one man, and death through sin, and in this way death came to all people, because all sinned—

To be sure, sin was in the world before the law was given, but sin is not charged against anyone's account where there is no law. Nevertheless, death reigned from the time of Adam to the time of Moses, even over those who did not sin by breaking a command, as did Adam, who is a pattern of the one to come.

But the gift is not like the trespass. For if the many died by the trespass of the one man, how much more did God's grace and the gift that came by the grace of the one man, Jesus Christ, overflow to the many! Nor can the gift of God be compared with the result of one man's sin: The judgment followed one sin and brought condemnation, but the gift followed many trespasses and brought justification. For if, by the trespass of the one man, death reigned through that one man, how much more will those who receive God's abundant provision of grace and of the gift of righteousness reign in life through the one man, Jesus Christ!

Consequently, just as one trespass resulted in condemnation for all people, so also one righteous act resulted in justification and life for all people. For just as through the disobedience of the one man the many were made sinners, so also through the obedience of the one man the many will be made righteous.

MEDITATION

All people are important to God. But all are deeply fallen. God's original perfect creation included flawless creatures with a spiritual and moral capacity. In the garden, they were given the ability to choose, so that they would be responding to God in a meaningful relationship. But choice always involves responsibility, and they were warned there would be consequences if they chose to disobey. Despite the richness of their relationship with God, they listened to a powerful evil being who came into their home. They fell to his tactics of doubt and deception. And they fell into sin by choosing their will over the Creator's. It is a mystery how beings who were created as moral and rational could succumb to the immorality of sin. But it happened, and it has left us in a constant battle and lifelong enmity with that serpent, that dragon, the devil.

The desire of the first two created beings to be like God led them to deny him and ignore his warning, and the consequences were heavy. There were ramifications in every area. There were physical and spiritual repercussions, and there was the separation—a great separation—from the Creator who had sustained them.

We are deeply fallen, yet we are greatly loved. The fall that took away our purity could not take away God's love for us. Nothing can. And so the need for the baby who was born on Christmas became inevitable, and the great plan was set in motion. The response of our holy and loving God to the disastrous effects of wickedness is ... surprisingly ... love.

PRAYER

Lord of all creation, I bow before you, recognizing that my deepest need is to be delivered from the bondage of evil that has ensnared me on account of my own sin. I readily confess that salvation is beyond my power. Thank you for refusing to leave me in this condition, choosing instead to send your Son, Jesus, to save me. Evil could not attach itself to him. He triumphed over the enemy and paid the penalty for my sin and the sin of all people with his death on the cross. I ask you to guide me in your ways and give me a clearer understanding of the blessings of obedience and the pain of disobedience so that I will grow in trust and take the risks I need to take in order to follow you completely. In Jesus' saving name I pray. Amen.   ✤

day3

GENESIS 12:1–3

The LORD had said to Abram, "Go from your country, your people and your father's household to the land I will show you. I will make you into a great nation, and I will bless you; I will make your name great, and you will be a blessing. I will bless those who bless you, and whoever curses you I will curse; and all peoples on earth will be blessed through you."

PSALM 86:9

All the nations you have made will come and worship before you, Lord; they will bring glory to your name.

ACTS 3:24–25

"Indeed, beginning with Samuel, all the prophets who have spoken have foretold these days. And you are heirs of the prophets and of the covenant God made with your fathers. He said to Abraham, 'Through your offspring all peoples on earth will be blessed.'"

GALATIANS 3:6–9,27–29

Abraham "believed God, and it was credited to him as righteousness." Understand, then, that those who have faith are children of Abraham. Scripture foresaw that God would justify the Gentiles by faith, and announced the gospel in advance to Abraham: "All na-

tions will be blessed through you." So those who rely
on faith are blessed along with Abraham, the man of
faith.

All of you who were baptized into Christ have
clothed yourselves with Christ. There is neither Jew
nor Gentile, neither slave nor free, nor is there male
and female, for you are all one in Christ Jesus. If you
belong to Christ, then you are Abraham's seed, and
heirs according to the promise.

ACTS 17:26–28

"From one man he made all the nations, that they
should inhabit the whole earth; and he marked out
their appointed times in history and the boundaries of
their lands. God did this so that they would seek him
and perhaps reach out for him and find him, though
he is not far from any one of us. 'For in him we live
and move and have our being.' As some of your own
poets have said, 'We are his offspring.'"

MEDITATION

God made a unilateral, unconditional covenant with Abraham, and ultimately, through Jesus, all believers get to
participate in the covenant. Abraham received a promise.
The promise to Abraham was not that he would be known
throughout all generations (though this has also become
true), but that all nations would be blessed, somehow,
through him. And just to make sure Abraham was not confused (and maybe so that we might not forget either), God
mentioned it four more times (see Genesis 18:18; 22:18;
26:4; 28:14)!

It was God's intention all along to bless all the people on earth. And he accomplished it, through a descendant of Abraham. Abraham did not celebrate Christmas. He did not know that Jesus was coming or that we would celebrate his great- great- great- ... grandson's birthday as a national holiday. He did not know that Jesus *was* the blessing; but he was. He is. And when we turn from our sin and put our faith in Jesus Christ as Lord, our life is hidden in him. We become heirs of the promise and heirs of God's promise. The call on our life, whether we realize and accept it or not, is to be used by God to bless all the nations of the earth. This is an enormous and serious responsibility. The fact that we've been invited to do it, and can actually do it, is cause for great joy. In being a blessing to the earth, we both become and fulfill the promise that God made to Abraham all those years ago.

PRAYER

Almighty God, thank you for fulfilling your promise to Abraham, sending your blessing to the whole world through your Son, Jesus Christ. Thank you for breaking down the walls that divide us from one another and from you. Thank you for making it possible for people from every race and culture to come to you through faith in your Son, Jesus, and for extending your grace and mercy to all people from every nation. Help me to know and to follow your ways even when they seem obscure to me. Open my eyes and my heart so that I can know you and your purposes. Guide me in my daily life that I might be a blessing to others by telling them of your great love. In Christ's glorious name I pray. Amen.♣

day⁴

PSALM 136:1–12,23–26

Give thanks to the LORD, for he is good.
His love endures forever.
Give thanks to the God of gods.
His love endures forever.
Give thanks to the Lord of lords:
His love endures forever.
to him who alone does great wonders,
His love endures forever.
who by his understanding made the heavens,
His love endures forever.
who spread out the earth upon the waters,
His love endures forever.
who made the great lights—
His love endures forever.
the sun to govern the day,
His love endures forever.
the moon and stars to govern the night;
His love endures forever.

to him who struck down the firstborn of Egypt
His love endures forever.
and brought Israel out from among them
His love endures forever.
with a mighty hand and outstretched arm;
His love endures forever.

He remembered us in our low estate
His love endures forever.

and freed us from our enemies.
His love endures forever.
He gives food to every creature.
His love endures forever.

Give thanks to the God of heaven.
His love endures forever.

JEREMIAH 31:3

"I have loved you with an everlasting love; I have drawn you with unfailing kindness."

JOHN 3:16

For God so loved the world that he gave his one and only Son, that whoever believes in him shall not perish but have eternal life.

1 JOHN 4:9–10

This is how God showed his love among us: He sent his one and only Son into the world that we might live through him. This is love: not that we loved God, but that he loved us and sent his Son as an atoning sacrifice for our sins.

MEDITATION

When someone is committed to us, it makes us feel secure. And when we involve ourselves in something that will last a long, long time, that makes us feel significant. God knows this and demonstrates his unshakable commitment to us — first. He offers us his grace and his acceptance. And he teaches us, gently and consistently, that his love endures forever. It is when we forget these two things that we fail and begin to believe the terrible lie that we are lovable only when we are great. We fall victim to this lie when all of our best efforts are done to be (or at least to look) great in order to win the attention and admiration of our peers.

But the clear teaching of Jesus is that we are loved because *God is great*, and it is on this we must depend. We need to realize that attempting to be who others want us to be and seeking their approval leaves us confused and lost. We need to learn that obedience to God's commands brings revelation and a personal knowledge of him, which fulfills even the deep longing of our heart for love, security and hope.

God sent a sign of his commitment to us — a gentle sign, a baby born. The best thing God had he gave to us. He sacrificed what was most precious to him in order to show us just how committed he is. And when we commit our lives to him, we see for ourselves that his love endures forever.

PRAYER

God of love, I bow in your presence, humbled and in awe of your astonishing love for me. Help me to remember that your love for me is my true security. Though I cannot fathom why you should commit yourself to me in the full knowledge of my sin, I thank you that you did. Though I cannot grasp why you should remain faithful when I have been so faithless, I praise you that you have. Though I cannot know why you would send your Son to suffer and die to rescue me and bring me back to you, with reverence and wonder I thank you for what you have done. Give me a greater ability to grasp the dimensions of your amazing love for me and fill my heart with this redeeming love so that something of your nature may be reflected in me, through Jesus Christ. Amen. ❖

dayˊ5

DEUTERONOMY 17:14–15,20

When you enter the land the LORD your God is giving you and have taken possession of it and settled in it, and you say, "Let us set a king over us like all the nations around us," be sure to appoint over you a king the LORD your God chooses. He must be from among your fellow Israelites. [He should] not consider himself better than his fellow Israelites and turn from the law to the right or to the left. Then he and his descendants will reign a long time over his kingdom in Israel.

MICAH 5:2–5

"But you, Bethlehem Ephrathah, though you are small ... out of you will come for me one who will be ruler over Israel, whose origins are from of old, from ancient times."

Therefore Israel will be abandoned until the time when she who is in labor bears a son, and the rest of his brothers return...

He will stand and shepherd his flock in the strength of the LORD, in the majesty of the name of the LORD his God. And they will live securely, for then his greatness will reach to the ends of the earth.

And he will be our peace.

REVELATION 19:11–16

I saw heaven standing open and there before me was a white horse, whose rider is called Faithful and True. With justice he judges and wages war. His eyes are like blazing fire, and on his head are many crowns. He has a name written on him that no one knows but he himself. He is dressed in a robe dipped in blood, and his name is the Word of God. The armies of heaven were following him, riding on white horses and dressed in fine linen, white and clean. Coming out of his mouth is a sharp sword with which to strike down the nations. "He will rule them with an iron scepter." He treads the winepress of the fury of the wrath of God Almighty. On his robe and on his thigh he has this name written: KING OF KINGS AND LORD OF LORDS.

MEDITATION

Jesus' greatness now reaches to the ends of the earth. And those who know him recognize him as faithful and true, one who has not taken his position by force (like so many earthly kings have), but who was chosen from before the beginning of time. And starting that day in Israel, the king first came as a baby, born into the line of Jewish nobility (because it was from among the Israelites that God had decreed a king would come), and yet from a long line of sinful people so he could identify with us and so that we would choose him too. This was the first time he came, not with force, but with the gentleness of an infant.

But the second time will be different. The second time, it will be sudden, and no one will miss it. Almighty God will open the gate of heaven, and Jesus will burst forth as a king, riding triumphant on a white stallion (not a donkey this time), with the armies of heaven following. Our great conquering king will destroy his enemies once and for all, waging and winning a holy war and ruling over all his people. Then he will reveal to a world that has rejected him that he truly is KING OF KINGS AND LORD OF LORDS. He will be absolutely sovereign over all people—the lost and the saved—and every knee will bow, and every tongue will confess that he is who we accept and claim that he is— Jesus, Christ, Lord.

PRAYER

Faithful Father, thank you for the hope of the second coming of Jesus Christ in glory and power. Help me to live in anticipation of his coming. Help me to trust you in the things I do not understand. And when life seems to be a mess, help me to remember that your work here on earth remains, for the time being, an unfinished project, and that you always complete what you begin. Help me to cultivate an eternal perspective as I journey through this temporal arena. May I learn to pursue the eternal reality of the unseen future over the current reality of the visible present. And may you always be the object of my deepest love so that I will pursue you above all else. In Christ's name I pray. Amen. ♣

day6

2 SAMUEL 7:5,16

"Go and tell my servant David, 'This is what the LORD says ... Your house and your kingdom will endure forever before me; your throne will be established forever.'"

PSALM 71:14–15

I will always have hope; I will praise you more and more. My mouth will tell of your righteous deeds, of your saving acts all day long.

ISAIAH 7:14

The Lord himself will give you a sign: The virgin will conceive and give birth to a son, and will call him Immanuel.

ISAIAH 9:1,7

There will be no more gloom for those who were in distress. Of the greatness of his government and peace there will be no end.

JEREMIAH 33:14–16

"'The days are coming,' declares the LORD, 'when I will fulfill the good promise I made to the people of Israel and Judah. In those days and at that time I will make a righteous Branch sprout from David's line; he will do what is just and right in the land. In those days Judah will be saved and Jerusalem will live in safety.

This is the name by which it will be called: The LORD Our Righteous Savior.'"

LUKE 2:14

"Glory to God in the highest heaven, and on earth peace to those on whom his favor rests."

MEDITATION

Throughout the Old Testament, God's people were waiting. Every struggle, every hardship could be endured because they believed that one day a Messiah was coming, and in the day of his coming, they would live in safety and freedom. Certainly, the Israelites did not understand exactly what this meant. They hoped for freedom from foreign oppression. But God's plan had to do with freedom from debt to sin. The bondage one feels when in financial debt is great and can lead to all kinds of trouble. How much greater is the debt people incur with acts of sin. It requires a sacrifice— loss of life. "For the wages of sin is death" (Romans 6:23). The Jews of Jesus' time knew this well; the temple floor ran red with the blood of offerings. The practice of making atonement was part of their culture.

But when Jesus suffered and died on the cross, as a sin offering, he paid that debt once for all. God is calling all people—all the slaves, all the prodigals, all the losers—to start over again on level ground. What a celebration we will have when we realize what this really means! This Christmas, before we go out and spend all of our money on the wants of this life, perhaps we should take a few minutes to thank the One who was born to pay all of our debts.

PRAYER

Generous and gracious heavenly Father, I confess that you have given me more than I could ever need. And yet, the more you give me, the more I want to keep for myself. The more you open your hands, the more I close mine to keep more. Help me to remember that I have been delivered from the crushing debt of sin. Thank you for sending your Son into the world to cancel my debt through his sacrifice and death on the cross. Help me to realize that your favor rests on me not because of anything I have done, but because of your mercy and your love. I pray in Jesus' name. Amen. ♣

day7

JUDGES 2:18

Whenever the LORD raised up a judge for them, he was with the judge and saved them out of the hands of their enemies as long as the judge lived; for the LORD relented because of their groaning under those who oppressed and afflicted them.

2 SAMUEL 22:2–4,7–10,17–20

"The LORD is my rock, my fortress and my
    deliverer;
    my God is my rock, in whom I take refuge,
    my shield and the horn of my salvation.
He is my stronghold, my refuge and my savior …
I called to the LORD, who is worthy of praise,
    and have been saved from my enemies.
In my distress I called to the LORD;
    I called out to my God.
From his temple he heard my voice;
    my cry came to his ears.
The earth trembled and quaked,
    the foundations of the heavens shook;
    they trembled because he was angry.
Smoke rose from his nostrils;
    consuming fire came from his mouth,
    burning coals blazed out of it.
He parted the heavens and came down …

He reached down from on high and took hold
of me;
he drew me out of deep waters.
He rescued me from my powerful enemy,
from my foes, who were too strong for me.
They confronted me in the day of my disaster,
but the LORD was my support.
He brought me out into a spacious place;
he rescued me because he delighted in me.

ISAIAH 11:1–4

A shoot will come up from the stump of Jesse;
from his roots a Branch will bear fruit.
The Spirit of the LORD will rest on him—
the Spirit of wisdom and of understanding,
the Spirit of counsel and of might,
the Spirit of the knowledge and fear of the
LORD—
and he will delight in the fear of the LORD.

He will not judge by what he sees with his eyes,
or decide by what he hears with his ears;
but with righteousness he will judge the needy,
with justice he will give decisions for the
poor of the earth.

PSALM 34:17–19

The righteous cry out, and the LORD hears them;
he delivers them from all their troubles. The LORD
is close to the brokenhearted and saves those who
are crushed in spirit. The righteous person may have

many troubles, but the LORD delivers him from them all.

ROMANS 10:13

"Everyone who calls on the name of the Lord will be saved."

MEDITATION

God had a plan all along to save his people and deliver them from their sins. The judges modeled the role of deliverer, but their work was always temporary. They may have been able to defeat an oppressive army who had conquered the Israelites, but they could not save the people from their own sinful tendencies; they couldn't even keep from sinning themselves.

But Jesus could. And the name Mary and Joseph gave their son — our sinless Savior — tells the whole story. The name *Jesus*, in Hebrew, means "Yahweh saves." There could be no clearer message. God is a saving God. Yet the problem the people in Jesus' time had in receiving Jesus is the same problem we face now. We all want a deliverer, someone to help us out of our financial struggles, our troubled relationships, our sickness. But no one can keep God's required end of the agreement. Instead of daily living for him, we break God's commandments and go our own way. We seek our own righteousness, ignoring the fact that the blood of a sacrificial death is required as payment for our sin.

Sin leads to bondage. Our God, who has control over all powers and authorities, over all of the spiritual forces in the world, over all of the rebellious people throughout the course of history, hears our cries for help. And nothing can stop him from saving us except our own foolish rejection of the deliverer himself.

PRAYER

Lord Jesus, you are my hope and my deliverer. In spite of my folly and waywardness, you hear my prayers and work in ways that are too marvelous for me to understand. I give thanks that you really care. Though I live in a broken world of sin, disease and death, I know that nothing can ever separate me from your love. In spite of the uncertainties of this life, I know that you will never leave or abandon me. You have set me free from the bondage of sin and death. May I freely lay hold of the benefits of prayer and seek your wisdom and power amid the adversities and uncertainties of this life. In your powerful and saving name I pray. Amen. ♣

day8

JEREMIAH 23:7–8

"The days are coming," declares the LORD, "when people will say … 'As surely as the LORD lives, who brought the descendants of Israel up out of the land of the north and out of all the countries where he had banished them.' Then they will live in their own land."

PROVERBS 3:13–18; 4:6,8

Blessed are those who find wisdom, those who gain understanding, for she is more profitable than silver and yields better returns than gold. She is more precious than rubies; nothing you desire can compare with her. Long life is in her right hand; in her left hand are riches and honor. Her ways are pleasant ways, and all her paths are peace. She is a tree of life to those who take hold of her; those who hold her fast will be blessed. Do not forsake wisdom, and she will protect you; love her, and she will watch over you. Cherish her, and she will exalt you; embrace her, and she will honor you.

1 CORINTHIANS 1:30

You are in Christ Jesus, who has become for us wisdom from God—that is, our righteousness, holiness and redemption.

COLOSSIANS 2:1–3

I want you to know how hard I am contending for you and for those at Laodicea, and for all who have not met me personally. My goal is that they may be encouraged in heart and united in love, so that they may have the full riches of complete understanding, in order that they may know the mystery of God, namely, Christ, in whom are hidden all the treasures of wisdom and knowledge.

JAMES 3:17

But the wisdom that comes from heaven is first of all pure; then peace-loving, considerate, submissive, full of mercy and good fruit, impartial and sincere.

MEDITATION

When the Bible speaks of wisdom, it does so in a very practical sense. Biblical wisdom is the skill required to live a well-ordered life. Wisdom must be cultivated. It is not a skill we are born with. There is, however, one notable exception, and Scripture is clear on this: Jesus Christ, the baby born in Bethlehem, is the wisdom of God personified. He is the skill of God at creation; he is the wise king promised by the prophets. He is wisdom come down from heaven, embodying peace and mercy and good fruit. He is the perfect revelation of the mysteries of God, pushing us beyond the limits of our own intelligence, crashing into the ceiling of our own comprehension.

The infant son of Mary and Joseph is the Son of God himself. And as he grows and as we get to know him better, we learn more. We see how he lives, never wavering from his intention of doing his Father's will, never allowing his human emotions to lead him into impulsiveness.

For us to become wise and live on solid ground, we must hear his words and put them into practice. All knowledge, all wisdom, everything we need to grow in life and godliness can be found in Jesus. We become his disciples. When we follow Jesus and live by his teachings, we gain wisdom to live as Jesus would have us live.

PRAYER

Jesus, I admit that I am often tempted to question your ways when they are contrary to what I want. Please open my eyes so that I will learn to follow you wherever you lead me. I submit to your authority, and I desire to trust you when I do not understand. Your words bring life — your message and wisdom surpass anything of this world. You have not only revealed the way I am to go but you also have provided me with the resources I need to travel along that way. I give thanks for the power of your indwelling Spirit, for your life-giving teaching and for the new quality of life to which you have called me. In your name I pray. Amen.   ✤

day 9

ISAIAH 42:1-7

"Here is my servant, whom I uphold,
  my chosen one in whom I delight;
I will put my Spirit on him,
  and he will bring justice to the nations.
He will not shout or cry out,
  or raise his voice in the streets.
A bruised reed he will not break,
  and a smoldering wick he will not snuff out.
In faithfulness he will bring forth justice;
  he will not falter or be discouraged
till he establishes justice on earth.
    In his teaching the islands will put their
      hope."
This is what God the LORD says—
the Creator of the heavens, who stretches
      them out,
  who spreads out the earth with all that
      springs from it,
  who gives breath to its people,
  and life to those who walk on it:
"I, the LORD, have called you in righteousness;
  I will take hold of your hand.
I will keep you and will make you
  to be a covenant for the people
  and a light for the Gentiles,

> to open eyes that are blind,
>> to free captives from prison
>> and to release from the dungeon those who
>>> sit in darkness."

MARK 10:45

"For even the Son of Man did not come to be served, but to serve, and to give his life as a ransom for many."

ROMANS 5:6–8

At just the right time, when we were still powerless, Christ died for the ungodly. Very rarely will anyone die for a righteous person, though for a good person someone might possibly dare to die. But God demonstrates his own love for us in this: While we were still sinners, Christ died for us."

MEDITATION

As the Suffering Servant of Isaiah, Jesus clearly communicated his purpose for coming to this earth: to serve. Jesus did not serve us *in spite of* his identity but rather *because of* his identity. Service is part of his very nature. His example of servanthood transcends any that has ever been seen before or since. Thus, in calling us to become like him, he calls us to join him in a lifestyle of service and sacrifice. Such service and sacrifice is not to be done *in spite of* our positions of leadership but, rather, precisely *because of* our positions of leadership: Such other-centered leadership, having been clearly modeled for us in the life of Jesus, is now our main calling. We are called not to be served in this world, but to serve and to give our lives away. Thus, by losing our life, we will discover it in its truest sense.

PRAYER

Lord Jesus, how humbling it is to know that you were willing to suffer and die on the cross for my sake. You were clear on why you had come and what you needed to do. You taught us to serve others and to love others and to always help the poor. You were never arrogant or unkind. Rather, you served selflessly. Help me to do better at serving others. Help me to forgive and not to seek revenge. Help me to love others, even my enemies. I pray that this understanding will become increasingly clear in my life. In your name I pray. Amen. ✤

day 10

PSALM 23:1–3

The LORD is my shepherd, I lack nothing. He makes me lie down in green pastures, he leads me beside quiet waters, he refreshes my soul. He guides me along the right paths for his name's sake.

ISAIAH 55:1–2

"Come, all you who are thirsty, come to the waters; and you who have no money, come, buy and eat! Come, buy wine and milk without money and without cost. Why spend money on what is not bread, and your labor on what does not satisfy? Listen, listen to me, and eat what is good, and you will delight in the richest of fare.

JOHN 4:7,9–11,13–14

When a Samaritan woman came to draw water, Jesus said to her, "Will you give me a drink?" The Samaritan woman said to him, "You are a Jew and I am a Samaritan woman. How can you ask me for a drink?" (For Jews do not associate with Samaritans.) Jesus answered her, "If you knew the gift of God and who it is that asks you for a drink, you would have asked him and he would have given you living water." "Sir," the woman said, "you have nothing to draw with and the well is deep. Where can you get this living water?" Jesus answered, "Everyone who drinks this water will be thirsty again, but whoever drinks the water I give them will never thirst. Indeed, the water I give them will become in them a spring of water welling up to eternal life."

JOHN 7:37–39

On the last and greatest day of the festival, Jesus stood and said in a loud voice, "Let anyone who is thirsty come to me and drink. Whoever believes in me, as Scripture has said, rivers of living water will flow from within them. By this he meant the Spirit, whom those who believed in him were later to receive.

REVELATION 7:17

"For the Lamb at the center of the throne will be their shepherd; 'he will lead them to springs of living water.' 'And God will wipe every tear from their eyes.'"

MEDITATION

When Adam and Eve were in the garden, every thirst was fully satisfied. But when they chose to disobey God, and sin entered the world, they found that things went horribly awry. Their relationship with one another soured. Their labor yielded frustration. Their health began to wane. They became thirsty, and this thirst has plagued humans ever since.

Then Jesus came into our world offering "living water." But at what cost? This is where the offer becomes almost unbelievable. Christ has chosen to give his water away to all who ask for it. And as part of the deal, he offers total forgiveness and reconciliation with God, redemption from our old futile way of life and a new pathway to purity and holiness. They are all within our grasp. All we must do is ask God, and we will receive the free gift of salvation. We need to open our hands, for even God cannot place his gift of salvation in a closed hand. The price Jesus is asking for this living water is zero—nothing.

Only our pride stands in our way. We must lay aside any idea that there is something that we can offer to God. We must ask him to give us what we do not have and cannot afford. That is the only basis on which the gift can be received. We must ask for it. Jesus is able to meet the deepest thirsts of the soul. In fact, that is precisely what he came to do.

PRAYER

Heavenly Father, I have longed for the living water only you can provide. And I praise your name that through your Son, Jesus Christ, I now have access to a spring of living water that promises to satisfy and lead me into abundant life. Allow that spring of water to flow out of my inner being and bear lasting fruit in the lives of others. I delight in the liberating truth that I do not need to earn this from you. I acknowledge the folly of even attempting such a thing! Give me the courage and strength to open my hands so that I may receive from you what it is you want to give me, for I know it will be more than I could ever ask for or imagine. By your grace, may I learn to live out of the resources you have given to me so that I will move forward in freedom as a true child of God. In Jesus' holy name I pray. Amen. ❖

day 11

EZEKIEL 34:11–15

"'For this is what the Sovereign LORD says: I myself will search for my sheep and look after them. As a shepherd looks after his scattered flock when he is with them, so will I look after my sheep. I will rescue them from all the places where they were scattered on a day of clouds and darkness. I will bring them out from the nations and gather them from the countries, and I will bring them into their own land. I will pasture them on the mountains of Israel, in the ravines and in all the settlements in the land. I will tend them in a good pasture, and the mountain heights of Israel will be their grazing land. There they will lie down in good grazing land, and there they will feed in a rich pasture on the mountains of Israel. I myself will tend my sheep and have them lie down, declares the Sovereign LORD.'"

PSALM 23:1

The LORD is my shepherd, I lack nothing.

MATTHEW 9:36

When [Jesus] saw the crowds, he had compassion on them, because they were harassed and helpless, like sheep without a shepherd.

JOHN 10:11,14–17,27–29

"I am the good shepherd. The good shepherd lays down his life for the sheep. I am the good shepherd;

I know my sheep and my sheep know me—just as the Father knows me and I know the Father—and I lay down my life for the sheep. I have other sheep that are not of this sheep pen. I must bring them also. They too will listen to my voice, and there shall be one flock and one shepherd. The reason my Father loves me is that I lay down my life—only to take it up again. My sheep listen to my voice; I know them, and they follow me. I give them eternal life, and they shall never perish; no one will snatch them out of my hand. My Father, who has given them to me, is greater than all; no one can snatch them out of my Father's hand.

1 PETER 2:25

For "you were like sheep going astray," but now you have returned to the Shepherd and Overseer of your souls.

MEDITATION

We are sheep: needy, defenseless, prone to wander and very stubborn. All people, even God's people, have been this way since the beginning of time. And there have always been wolves for whom a lone sheep is an easy target. This is why God has a *people* and not a *person*—why we are told to stick together. Together, we need a shepherd.

When we believe in Jesus, the Father gives us into the hands of the Shepherd he promised and sent at just the right time—the time we now remember in history as Christmas. And our Shepherd is good. He is noble and trustworthy. He guides his sheep and does not drive us. He knows us intimately, knows each one of our names and never fails to lead us on the right path. He protects us. He gathers us in, always looking for the one who is lost, the one outside the fold of his care.

There are those who would steal and kill the sheep for their own purposes. This is why we must listen to what the Good Shepherd says and learn to discern his words: "That sounds like something Jesus would say" or "That does not." We are to stay in his flock, with other believers, never wandering away from it, because together with the other sheep, we can follow the Shepherd's lead. We can stay very, very close to him. Then no one can snatch us out of his hand, and we will live with him forever.

PRAYER

Jesus, you are the good Shepherd, caring for me and giving me rest, correcting me when I stray, tending my wounds and protecting me from my enemies. I confess that I am weak-willed and prone to wander. Yet you never give up on me. You refuse to abandon me—even when I have brought calamity upon myself.

Teach me the joy of surrender and the blessings of obedience. Help me to willingly submit to your lordship in every area of my life, to obey your teachings. Guide me in doing the work you have set out for me to do. I love you. My hope is in you, my trust is in you. May I learn to discern your voice so that I may live in obedience to your will right up to the day of your glorious return. In your name I pray. Amen. ♣

day 12

LUKE 1:5–20,22,24

In the time of Herod king of Judea there was a priest named Zechariah, who belonged to the priestly division of Abijah; his wife Elizabeth was also a descendant of Aaron. Both of them were righteous in the sight of God, observing all the Lord's commands and decrees blamelessly. But they were childless because Elizabeth was not able to conceive, and they were both very old.

Once when Zechariah's division was on duty and he was serving as priest before God, he was chosen by lot, according to the custom of the priesthood, to go into the temple of the Lord and burn incense. And when the time for the burning of incense came, all the assembled worshipers were praying outside.

Then an angel of the Lord appeared to him, standing at the right side of the altar of incense. When Zechariah saw him, he was startled and was gripped with fear. But the angel said to him: "Do not be afraid, Zechariah; your prayer has been heard. Your wife Elizabeth will bear you a son, and you are to call him John. He will be a joy and delight to you, and many will rejoice because of his birth, for he will be great in the sight of the Lord. He is never to take wine or other fermented drink, and he will be filled with the Holy Spirit even before he is born. He will bring back many of the people of Israel to the Lord their

God. And he will go on before the Lord, in the spirit
and power of Elijah, to turn the hearts of the parents
to their children and the disobedient to the wisdom
of the righteous — to make ready a people prepared
for the Lord."

Zechariah asked the angel, "How can I be sure of
this? I am an old man and my wife is well along in
years."

The angel said to him, "I am Gabriel. I stand in
the presence of God, and I have been sent to speak
to you and to tell you this good news. And now you
will be silent and not able to speak until the day this
happens, because you did not believe my words, which
will come true at their appointed time."

When he came out, he could not speak to them.
They realized he had seen a vision in the temple, for
he kept making signs to them but remained unable to
speak.

After this his wife Elizabeth became pregnant and
for five months remained in seclusion.

MEDITATION

In the days and months preceding the birth of Jesus Christ,
things were predictable in that area of the world. Though
Herod the Great had ordered some upgrades to the temple,
daily worship and ritual did not cease. Twenty-four divisions
of priests rotated on a timetable like gears in a Swiss watch.
What happened each day was what was expected to happen.

But then an unexpected event occurred that disrupted
the well-ordered world of one priest and his wife and led to
a series of unexpected events that would eventually disrupt

our world too. Zechariah and his wife suffered unfulfilled longings. Though they were faithful servants of God, they had to endure the pain and disgrace of childlessness.

But Zechariah didn't let his disappointments keep him from service. He did not get distracted from his duties to the Lord and to his community. And when a literal luck of the draw won him a turn in the holiest place of all, an angel appeared and promised his heart's desire. God would override nature (as he had with Abraham and Sarah before) to prove his faithfulness. Elizabeth, a senior citizen, would bear a child. Their years of waiting and watching and hoping and praying would find their fulfillment in the birth of a son, a very special son.

As we grapple with our own unfulfilled yearnings and unmet needs, may we remember that the events of so long ago echo in our lives today. We still long for fulfillment; we still desire someone who will meet our needs. In Zechariah's and Elizabeth's blessing of their son John, the herald of the one to come, we see the answer to our own struggles. God will provide. God will send his Son.

PRAYER

Dear Lord, I confess that I am often impatient with the processes of this world. My resources, wisdom and power are so limited that I control very few of the things that happen in my life. I grow frustrated with the challenges and unexpected troubles that crop up so often. But when I think more deeply, I realize that these setbacks and circumstances can accomplish more to shape my character than having everything go my way. It is through such difficulties that patience, steadfastness and fortitude are forged by your wise and loving hands. May I learn to wait on you, to hope in you, to trust in you, to delight myself in you and to unreservedly commit my ways to you. In your Son's name I pray. Amen.   ❖

day 13

LUKE 1:26–38,46–55

In the sixth month of Elizabeth's pregnancy, God sent the angel Gabriel to Nazareth, a town in Galilee, to a virgin pledged to be married to a man named Joseph, a descendant of David. The virgin's name was Mary. The angel went to her and said, "Greetings, you who are highly favored! The Lord is with you."

Mary was greatly troubled at his words and wondered what kind of greeting this might be. But the angel said to her, "Do not be afraid, Mary; you have found favor with God. You will conceive and give birth to a son, and you are to call him Jesus. He will be great and will be called the Son of the Most High. The Lord God will give him the throne of his father David, and he will reign over Jacob's descendants forever; his kingdom will never end."

"How will this be," Mary asked the angel, "since I am a virgin?"

The angel answered, "The Holy Spirit will come on you, and the power of the Most High will overshadow you. So the holy one to be born will be called the Son of God. Even Elizabeth your relative is going to have a child in her old age, and she who was said to be unable to conceive is in her sixth month. For no word from God will ever fail."

"I am the Lord's servant," Mary answered. "May your word to me be fulfilled." Then the angel left her.

And Mary said: "My soul glorifies the Lord and my spirit rejoices in God my Savior, for he has been mindful of the humble state of his servant. From now on all generations will call me blessed, for the Mighty One has done great things for me—holy is his name. His mercy extends to those who fear him, from generation to generation. He has performed mighty deeds with his arm; he has scattered those who are proud in their inmost thoughts. He has brought down rulers from their thrones but has lifted up the humble. He has filled the hungry with good things but has sent the rich away empty. He has helped his servant Israel, remembering to be merciful to Abraham and his descendants forever, just as he promised our ancestors."

JAMES 4:6

"God opposes the proud but shows favor to the humble."

MEDITATION

An angel makes outrageous promises to Mary. He tells her, "No word from God will ever fail." And that was enough for her. "May your word to me be fulfilled," she said. We wonder at her words. How could she be so calm and stoic? She had to be terrified. Mary knew there would be smirks and whispers when people found out about her unplanned pregnancy; by law, she could be stoned to death. A weak person would not have responded the way she did. But what if "terrified" gave way to "trust" as the word of the Lord came to her through this angel? What if "May your word to

me be fulfilled" really means "Let's do this!" Though she
may not have understood the details, she was assured that
the long-awaited Messiah would come through her—God
was giving her his word. And that was enough. Mary began
to worship.

There is a joy that follows a difficult submission to God,
a joy that will have to be remembered and held onto when
the long obedience becomes nearly unbearable. It is what
sustains us and compels us to worship in the midst of deep
suffering, to find companionship with the One who suffered
everything for our sakes.

That is what led Mary to break forth in song, a song
we today call the "Magnificat." Because Mary endured, the
Son that came after the song has sustained generations of
humble worshipers, like Mary, ever since.

PRAYER

*O Lord, you are God of the unexpected. Just when I think
I have a clear idea where things are heading, you appear
and intervene in the most astonishing and creative ways.
When this happens, I am reminded again that my field of
vision is so limited that I can only see as far as the first bend
in the road ahead. You have said that my faith in you is
the assurance of things hoped for, the conviction of things
not seen. When I hope in you, I hope in what I do not see,
and I pray that I will persevere in waiting eagerly for the
realization of all that you have promised. To trust in what
you call me to do and to obey your direction often does not
make sense to my eyes. Nevertheless, having come to faith
in Christ Jesus, I know that I have no other viable option*

than to echo Mary's words: "I am the Lord's servant. May your word to me be fulfilled." I humbly pray that I will be able to complete whatever task you give to me. In Jesus' name I pray. Amen.   ✤

day 14

LUKE 1:57–66,80

When it was time for Elizabeth to have her baby, she gave birth to a son.... On the eighth day [her neighbors and relatives] came to circumcise the child, and they were going to name him after his father Zechariah, but his mother spoke up and said, "No! He is to be called John."

They said to her, "There is no one among your relatives who has that name."

Then they made signs to his father, to find out what he would like to name the child. He asked for a writing tablet, and to everyone's astonishment he wrote, "His name is John." Immediately his mouth was opened and his tongue set free, and he began to speak, praising God. All the neighbors were filled with awe, and throughout the hill country of Judea people were talking about all these things. Everyone who heard this wondered about it, asking, "What then is this child going to be?" For the Lord's hand was with him.

And the child grew and became strong in spirit; and he lived in the wilderness until he appeared publicly to Israel.

LUKE 3:3–6

He went into all the country around the Jordan, preaching a baptism of repentance for the forgiveness

of sins. As it is written in the book of the words of
Isaiah the prophet:

> "A voice of one calling in the wilderness,
> 'Prepare the way for the Lord,
>   make straight paths for him.
> Every valley shall be filled in,
>   every mountain and hill made low.
> The crooked roads shall become straight,
>   the rough ways smooth.
> And all people will see God's salvation.'"

JOHN 1:6–9,15

There was a man sent from God whose name was
John. He came as a witness to testify concerning that
light, so that through him all might believe. He himself was not the light; he came only as a witness to the
light.

The true light that gives light to everyone was
coming into the world.

(John testified concerning him. He cried out, saying, "This is the one I spoke about when I said, 'He
who comes after me has surpassed me because he was
before me.'")

MEDITATION

A king was on his way. And they might have missed him,
the king who would fulfill Old Testament prophecy and become the main subject of the New Testament. So John was
sent as a herald. John is the bridge, the threshold between

what had been and what was about to be. He is the precursor, the forerunner, the opening act, the appointed messenger, carrying the promise that the centuries of waiting and preparing and anticipating were about to come to a great and glorious fulfillment. In John, the prophecies began to be fulfilled. And a few people understood it—the early adopters, those quick to catch on. But even to these, his own disciples, he pointed to Jesus, the one whose sandal he was unfit to tie.

As great as the teaching of John the Baptist was, it was nothing compared to Jesus' teaching. And how well John the Baptist understood his role and stuck to it. What amazing clarity of purpose. Yet we can learn from him too. We can learn that preparation for the Messiah (then as now) requires a conversion and a transformation of the heart and mind. We can learn that the focus is not on us or on anything that we have done or hope to do, not even if it is for God. We can learn that our job, like John's, is to spread the Good News, to point all people to behold Jesus and to seek his message of salvation.

PRAYER

Holy Father, your grace humbles me without degrading me and elevates me without inflating me. You offer me great dignity and worth; without you I am nothing and have nothing. I am grateful that you have given me the astounding invitation to participate in something that extends so far beyond me, though I really have little to offer. I can only revel in your kindness, grace and compassion.

I know that you can accomplish what is needed in your plan without me, and yet you invite me to participate in what will last forever. I ask you to guide me and to teach me how to fulfill your unique purposes for my life. I pray that, by your grace, I will become the person you created me to be, accomplishing the works you have prepared beforehand for me. In your Son's precious name I pray. Amen. ✤

day15

MATTHEW 1:17–25

There were fourteen generations in all from Abraham to David, fourteen from David to the exile to Babylon, and fourteen from the exile to the Messiah.

This is how the birth of Jesus the Messiah came about: His mother Mary was pledged to be married to Joseph, but before they came together, she was found to be pregnant through the Holy Spirit. Because Joseph her husband was faithful to the law, and yet did not want to expose her to public disgrace, he had in mind to divorce her quietly.

But after he had considered this, an angel of the Lord appeared to him in a dream and said, "Joseph son of David, do not be afraid to take Mary home as your wife, because what is conceived in her is from the Holy Spirit. She will give birth to a son, and you are to give him the name Jesus, because he will save his people from their sins."

All this took place to fulfill what the Lord had said through the prophet: "The virgin will conceive and give birth to a son, and they will call him Immanuel" (which means "God with us").

When Joseph woke up, he did what the angel of the Lord had commanded him and took Mary home as his wife. But he did not consummate their marriage until she gave birth to a son. And he gave him the name Jesus.

MEDITATION

Before Mary got pregnant, Joseph had an impeccable repu-
tation. That is not something to be taken lightly. He had
spent his life becoming a *tsadiq*, a righteous man. He studied the Torah; he obeyed its precepts. He recited every day,
"Hear O Israel ... the Lord thy God is one God ..." He followed food laws and knew to love the Lord his God with all
his heart and soul and mind and strength.

Now he had to make a choice: to stand by his betrothed,
who had somehow gotten pregnant, or maintain the repu-
tation he had spent a lifetime earning. There was no keeping both. But all of that Torah he had internalized had made
him forgiving, grace-filled and committed to a strict obedience to the call of God.

Joseph was preparing to divorce Mary, to disengage from
her in the gentlest way possible, when an angel entered the
scene and delivered a message from God that confirmed
what Mary was saying about the baby. And though no one
will believe him, Joseph sacrifices everything and follows
the call of God. Yes, people will talk about him, whether
the baby is his or not. But Joseph has chosen the approval
of God over the approval of people—the best choice he
ever made.

PRAYER

*Lord God, as I read the stories of the Bible, I see again and
again that you call your people to do things that, at the time,
do not seem to make any sense. I also realize that the reason
your will did not make sense to them is that our vision is
limited—we cannot see the end you have in mind. I cannot*

even know what my own best interests look like because I would need to know the future, and only you know that. Because my perspective is so limited, help me to learn to trust you and do what you ask me to do because I know that will always work out for my greater good. And as trust helps me to overcome fear, may I learn to risk everything as I work to fulfill the purposes that you have assigned to me. In Christ's name I pray. Amen.   ❖

day 16

ISAIAH 9:6

For to us a child is born, to us a son is given, and the government will be on his shoulders. And he will be called Wonderful Counselor, Mighty God, Everlasting Father, Prince of Peace.

MARK 1:4,7–8

John the Baptist appeared in the wilderness, preaching a baptism of repentance for the forgiveness of sins. And this was his message: "After me comes the one more powerful that I ... I baptize you with water, but he will baptize you with the Holy Spirit."

LUKE 2:1–7

In those days Caesar Augustus issued a decree that a census should be taken of the entire Roman world. (This was the first census that took place while Quirinius was governor of Syria.) And everyone went to their own town to register.

So Joseph also went up from the town of Nazareth in Galilee to Judea, to Bethlehem the town of David, because he belonged to the house and line of David. He went there to register with Mary, who was pledged to be married to him and was expecting a child. While they were there, the time came for the baby to be born, and she gave birth to her firstborn, a son. She wrapped him in cloths and placed him in a manger, because there was no guest room available for them.

MEDITATION

God does things we would never think of. And he does things in ways we think would never work. But God's ways are so much wiser than any of our plans. Imagine if God had chosen to come to earth as a grown man. He then might have been more of what his people were expecting as they looked for the Messiah that had been promised. But a baby? How can a child, who is helpless and totally dependent, be the Messiah?

None of what happened that day in that stable, among the animals, was grand. God the Father gave his Son a completely humble birth and an almost regular childhood. "And the child grew and became strong; he was filled with wisdom, and the grace of God was on him" (Luke 2:40).

And, against all kinds of opposition, this tiny baby will be the one to save our lives and someday rule the world. It doesn't make much sense to us. A baby? But that is because we are so limited in our understanding of the ways of God.

Still, do not miss this vitally important lesson: The God of the universe is content to use the weak things of the world to confound the strong. And this truth should give us comfort. If he can use a baby to change the world, he can certainly use us.

PRAYER

Father God, your kingdom ways appear to be upside down to me, but I am beginning to see that it is my vision that is distorted. The mystery of the incarnation is utterly unique in the history of the world—the God becoming flesh in order to become one of us. The radical and profound lengths to which you went in order to save us all from the power of Satan amazes me. As I read the story of the first Advent, I am struck by all that you put into place. Only you could have conceived of it. Having made the world, you sent your Son into the world, knowing that he would be betrayed, rejected and crucified by the people he came to save. And yet you did it—to save me. I praise your name and thank you for your awesome gift of salvation. In Jesus' name I pray. Amen. ✤

day 17

LUKE 2:8-20

And there were shepherds living out in the fields nearby, keeping watch over their flocks at night. An angel of the Lord appeared to them, and the glory of the Lord shone around them, and they were terrified. But the angel said to them, "Do not be afraid. I bring you good news that will cause great joy for all the people. Today in the town of David a Savior has been born to you; he is the Messiah, the Lord. This will be a sign to you: You will find a baby wrapped in cloths and lying in a manger."

Suddenly a great company of the heavenly host appeared with the angel, praising God and saying,

> "Glory to God in the highest heaven,
> and on earth peace to those on whom his favor rests."

When the angels had left them and gone into heaven, the shepherds said to one another, "Let's go to Bethlehem and see this thing that has happened, which the Lord has told us about."

So they hurried off and found Mary and Joseph, and the baby, who was lying in the manger. When they had seen him, they spread the word concerning what had been told them about this child, and all who heard it were amazed at what the shepherds said to them. But Mary treasured up all these things and pondered them in her heart. The shepherds returned, glorifying and praising God for all the things they had heard and seen, which were just as they had been told.

MEDITATION

Shepherds spent their days alone, living outside in the fields among the animals. Their job was a basic-level job; in Jesus' time, it was not, and is not now, a prestigious position. Shepherds were not celebrated people. They were largely ignored. But they had one quality that was very special. They were watchful, especially at night. It was their job to be watchful.

Shepherds in the fields were the first ones told about the birth of Jesus that night. Maybe they were the only ones awake when God decided to reveal his big surprise with his unbelievable angelic announcement. Or maybe God chose these lowly working shepherds to show us that he loves all people. He doesn't care about wealth or fame or position in society.

And so the shepherds became the first witnesses and worshipers. This greatest of all worship services began out in the fields, in front of a flock of fuzzy, stinky animals, among a group of humble, faithful worshipers who then spread the news of the Shepherd who had come to save all people.

PRAYER

Dear Lord, I praise and bless your name for the limitless magnitude of your love in sending your Son, the Lamb of God, who takes away the sins of the world. And I am unspeakably grateful that you sent your angels to announce the birth of our Savior to the lowly shepherds on that first Christmas. I thank you that there are no preconditions or qualifications that we are required to achieve before worshiping Jesus. Instead, we can come as we are in all our uncleanness and corruption, and humbly receive the gift of life that we could never merit. I am grateful that whoever will call on the name of the Lord will be saved. May I always be thankful for your glorious gift and recall the terrible price you paid to make it possible. In your Son's name I humbly pray. Amen. ❖

day 18

JOB 38:4–7

"Where were you when I laid the earth's foundation? Tell me, if you understand. Who marked off its dimensions? Surely you know! Who stretched a measuring line across it? On what were its footings set, or who laid its cornerstone—while the morning stars sang together and all the angels shouted for joy?

ROMANS 8:38–39

For I am convinced that neither death nor life, neither angels nor demons, neither the present nor the future, nor any powers, neither height nor depth, nor anything else in all creation, will be able to separate us from the love of God that is in Christ Jesus our Lord.

ROMANS 12:16

Do not be proud, but be willing to associate with people of low position. Do not be conceited.

1 PETER 1:10–12

Concerning this salvation, the prophets, who spoke of the grace that was to come to you, searched intently and with the greatest care, trying to find out the time and circumstances to which the Spirit of Christ in them was pointing when he predicted the sufferings of the Messiah and the glories that would follow. It was revealed to them that they were not serving themselves but you, when they spoke of the things that have now been told you by those who have preached the gospel to you by the Holy Spirit sent from heaven. Even angels long to look into these things.

MEDITATION

The angels rejoiced at the beginning of time, reveling in God's awesome creation, perhaps the most beautiful thing they had ever seen. How sad it must have been, later, for the two of them who were chosen to guard the garden gate against reentry by those two people whose sins we are all now born into. But the angels, because they live in his presence, know the character of God. And so they waited. They longed to look into the mysterious promises that the prophets were bringing, the coming grace of God, but they were mostly silent. They longed for the day of our redemption, yet they were mostly invisible. They sometimes appeared, one or two at a time, throughout the Old Testament when God sent them as messengers or sometimes as heavenly hosts in great spiritual battles. But mostly they waited ... eagerly.

So when one of them was sent to tell the shepherds that the news of God's grace had reached them too, that a baby had been born, the Messiah, who would bring great joy to all people, the angels could remain quiet no longer. All heaven broke loose. And for a moment, in that field, the supernatural broke through the barrier of our natural world in a glorious celebration of our salvation.

Before we knew that God was coming for us, the angels knew. And they interrupted our earthly monotony with song: "Glory to God in the highest heaven, and on earth peace to those on whom his favor rests" (Luke 2:14). What was so wonderful to the angels that they could not restrain their adoration should be a wonder to us too. This Christmas, let us remember that the miracle of our salvation is truly that, a great and glorious miracle, one that sent angels into glorious raptures of praise. And let us pray that our God will interrupt our lives with the joy of this message, just as he did for those shepherds in the field.

PRAYER

Lord God, you are the sovereign, majestic and transcendent ruler of all things, both visible and invisible, past and present. The angelic hosts of heaven serve you continually to accomplish your perfect will. Break into our lives, interrupt our routines, open our blinded eyes and stir our calloused hearts to reveal how amazing your plan truly is. I recognize that in this life I see so little and know only part. Yet the time is coming when I will see you face to face. The joy of my salvation is my strength. In your holy name I pray. Amen. ✤

day 19

MATTHEW 2:1–12

After Jesus was born in Bethlehem in Judea, during the time of King Herod, Magi from the east came to Jerusalem and asked, "Where is the one who has been born king of the Jews? We saw his star when it rose and have come to worship him."

When King Herod heard this he was disturbed, and all Jerusalem with him. When he had called together all the people's chief priests and teachers of the law, he asked them where the Messiah was to be born. "In Bethlehem in Judea," they replied, "for this is what the prophet has written: "'But you, Bethlehem, in the land of Judah, are by no means least among the rulers of Judah; for out of you will come a ruler who will shepherd my people Israel.'"

Then Herod called the Magi secretly and found out from them the exact time the star had appeared. He sent them to Bethlehem and said, "Go and search carefully for the child. As soon as you find him, report to me, so that I too may go and worship him."

After they had heard the king, they went on their way, and the star they had seen when it rose went ahead of them until it stopped over the place where the child was. When they saw the star, they were overjoyed. On coming to the house, they saw the child with his mother Mary, and they bowed down and worshiped him. Then they opened their treasures and presented him with gifts of gold, frankincense and myrrh. And having been warned in a dream not to go back to Herod, they returned to their country by another route.

PSALM 72:10–11

May the kings of Tarshish and of distant shores bring tribute to him. May the kings of Sheba and Seba present him gifts. May all kings bow down to him and all nations serve him.

MEDITATION

All of our Christmas cards and songs picture the Magi appearing at the manger and laying gifts at the feet of a tiny baby. But Scripture is clear that this is not how it happened. The Magi made a journey of nearly 900 dangerous miles, likely traversing Persia, traveling across the Arabian desert, arriving first in Jerusalem and never giving up until reaching the place where they would find the promised king—in a small house in Bethlehem.

They were searching for the king of the Jews (though not Jews themselves) by following a star in the east. By the time they arrived, the baby probably was near toddler size and growing. It had to have taken some measure of faith to believe what the star was indicating, that this tiny house held the greatest king to ever live and then that this little child was the king they sought. But when they entered, they worshiped, laying down everything that they had carried for so long.

These courageous and obedient pilgrims show something amazing about God that he likely does not want us to miss. They were not Jews. They were wise men from a far-off land who had studied for years and traveled for months to find a special king. These outsiders sought a Messiah, just like the Jews whose hearts longed for his coming, and God did not deny them what they were seeking. What a perfect picture of those who seek Christ with all their heart. All who seek him find him, even if they have to cross a desert and endure months or years of a pilgrimage to do so.

PRAYER

Father in heaven, you have graciously revealed rich and wonderful truths about your nature and plan that we could never have known on our own. The heavens declare the glory of your invisible attributes—your eternal power and divine nature. But nothing in your created order could prepare us for the revelation that the God of majesty and sovereign glory sent his only Son to be born into a modest peasant family. This sacrifice made it possible for us to enjoy a loving relationship with you through the merits of your glorious Son. What we could never learn in nature, you have revealed in your Word, which centers on the Person and work of Christ Jesus, the Alpha and the Omega. May I learn to humble myself and respond in love and obedience to the Lord Jesus, who has given himself to rescue and draw me to you, and may I become more like him in my spiritual journey. In Jesus' name I pray. Amen.   ✣

day20

MATTHEW 2:13–16,19–23

When [the Magi] had gone, an angel of the Lord appeared to Joseph in a dream. "Get up," he said, "take the child and his mother and escape to Egypt. Stay there until I tell you, for Herod is going to search for the child to kill him."

So he got up, took the child and his mother during the night and left for Egypt, where he stayed until the death of Herod. And so was fulfilled what the Lord had said through the prophet: "Out of Egypt I called my son."

When Herod realized that he had been outwitted by the Magi, he was furious, and he gave orders to kill all the boys in Bethlehem and its vicinity who were two years old and under, in accordance with the time he had learned from the Magi.

After Herod died, an angel of the Lord appeared in a dream to Joseph in Egypt and said, "Get up, take the child and his mother and go to the land of Israel, for those who were trying to take the child's life are dead."

So he got up, took the child and his mother and went to the land of Israel. But when he heard that Archelaus was reigning in Judea in place of his father Herod, he was afraid to go there. Having been warned in a dream, he withdrew to the district of Galilee, and he went and lived in a town called Nazareth. So was fulfilled what was said through the prophets, that he would be called a Nazarene.

LUKE 2:25–32

Now there was a man in Jerusalem called Simeon, who was righteous and devout. It had been revealed to him by the Holy Spirit that he would not die before he had seen the Lord's Messiah. Moved by the Spirit, he went into the temple courts. When the parents brought in the child Jesus ... Simeon took him in his arms and praised God, saying:

"Sovereign Lord, as you have promised,
>   you may now dismiss your servant in peace.
For my eyes have seen your salvation,
>   which you have prepared in the sight of all
>   nations:
a light for revelation to the Gentiles,
>   and the glory of your people Israel."

MEDITATION

Herod was a cruel and illegitimate king. He was a pretender who used manipulation to ascend to the throne because he knew he was not actually entitled to be king. And here is the thing about using manipulation to get anything: If we use manipulation to get power, we will have to use it to maintain that power. And so Herod did, accomplishing his purposes through intimidation, murder and a feigning and false submission to those who would determine if he would remain.

So it should come as no surprise that news of the birth of a rightful heir to the throne frightens Herod and inspires even greater evil. The arrival of the wise men brought an opportunity for Herod, a chance to repent and humble himself in worship to the true newborn king. And this is what he claims to want to do. But he has so trained himself in evil and so loves what he struggles to hold on to (and will, consequently, lose) that he cannot bring himself to worship.

We are all pretenders to some "throne." We manipulate to keep relationships in check. We hold on to things that are not legitimately ours. We try to cover our sins. But there is always a choice: to cling to our power (though it will inevitably be lost) or to cling to the One who is our true King, to surrender all to the One who can make our motives pure again.

PRAYER

Living God, may I never place my security in status or the approval of others, but only in you, in your character and promises. Deliver me from insecurity and anxiety that can cripple me and erode my faith in you. I want to be increasingly defined by your truth and not by the lies of a fleeting and broken world. May I be your person, even in times of trouble and stress, knowing that from you and through you and to you are all things.

As I cast all my anxiety on you, help me to experience your peace and make choices that are honoring to you instead of foolish decisions that spring from fear and disbelief. Thank you for the grace of forgiveness when I do things that are displeasing to you. I am grateful that there is no sin so great that it would prevent you from welcoming me back when I come to my senses and return to you. In your Son's great and holy name I pray. Amen. ❧

day21

ISAIAH 35:4–6

Say to those with fearful hearts, "Be strong, do not fear; your God will come, he will come with vengeance; with divine retribution he will come to save you." Then will the eyes of the blind be opened and the ears of the deaf unstopped. Then will the lame leap like a deer, and the mute tongue shout for joy. Water will gush forth in the wilderness and streams in the desert.

ISAIAH 53:4–5

Surely he took up our pain and bore our suffering, yet we considered him punished by God, stricken by him, and afflicted. But he was pierced for our transgressions, he was crushed for our iniquities; the punishment that brought us peace was on him, and by his wounds we are healed.

MALACHI 4:2

"But for you who revere my name, the sun of righteousness will rise with healing in its rays. And you will go out and frolic like well-fed calves."

MATTHEW 4:23

Jesus went throughout Galilee, teaching in their synagogues, proclaiming the good news of the kingdom, and healing every disease and sickness among the people.

MATTHEW 9:20–22

A woman who had been subject to bleeding for twelve years came up behind him and touched the edge of his cloak. She said to herself, "If I only touch his cloak, I will be healed." Jesus turned and saw her. "Take heart, daughter," he said, "your faith has healed you." And the woman was healed at that moment.

JOHN 11:45–48

Therefore many of the Jews who had come to visit Mary, and had seen what Jesus did, believed in him. But some of them went to the Pharisees and told them what Jesus had done. Then the chief priests and the Pharisees called a meeting of the Sanhedrin.

"What are we accomplishing?" they asked. "Here is this man performing many signs. If we let him go on like this, everyone will believe in him, and then the Romans will come and take away both our temple and our nation."

MARK 12:24

Jesus replied, "Are you not in error because you do not know the Scriptures or the power of God?"

MEDITATION

Jesus' life began as a miracle. Virgins do not give birth to babies. Jesus' deliverance from Herod's infanticide could be another miracle. And then consider the flight to Egypt and the return to Nazareth. The way Jesus grew up, the depth of knowledge he showed at such an early age in the temple—perhaps these were miracles as well.

And then when people began to suspect that he was more than just a traveling rabbi, they asked him, "Are you the expected one, or should we look for someone else?" His answer was simple: "Look at the things I am doing." Blind people gained their sight. Crippled people straightened up and leaped for joy. Sometimes he healed with a word or a touch. Sometimes he wasn't even present; he healed from a distance. Food seemed to materialize out of thin air and thousands feasted until their bellies were full. Miracle after miracle validated the message and person of Jesus until no one could deny his power over creation, over disease, over demons, over death itself.

Jesus' miracles were proof that God was with him, proof for the skeptics who would not otherwise realize that he was the One sent by God. More importantly, the miracles added to the mounting evidence that he had the power to forgive sins.

Seeing miracles today may be a matter of refining our definition of the word itself, knowing what to look for and understanding the purpose of God's miraculous activity. When we open our hearts and minds to such activity, we need to remember that God's purpose is not merely to help people. He means for us to look beyond the miracle—to the Miracle Worker himself.

PRAYER

Lord Jesus, the Gospels proclaim the abundance of marvelous things you said and did during your brief public ministry. You made claims no one had ever made before or since, and you had the authority to back up those claims by your extraordinary works. Yet you did all this in a context of profound humility, never calling attention to yourself, but instead pointing to your heavenly Father. Thank you for breathing new life and strength into me to make me a new creation in your kingdom. Open my eyes to see your glory as I wait in anticipation for the day when I will receive a resurrected body that will be in conformity with the body of your glory. In your powerful name I pray. Amen. ❖

day22

JOHN 1:14–18

The Word became flesh and made his dwelling
among us. We have seen his glory, the glory of the
one and only Son, who came from the Father, full of
grace and truth.

(John testified concerning him. He cried out, saying, "This is the one I spoke about when I said, 'He
who comes after me has surpassed me because he was
before me.'") Out of his fullness we have all received
grace in place of grace already given. For the law was
given through Moses; grace and truth came through
Jesus Christ. No one has ever seen God, but the one
and only Son, who is himself God and is in closest
relationship with the Father, has made him known.

ACTS 3:19–22

"Repent, then, and turn to God, so that your sins
may be wiped out, that times of refreshing may come
from the Lord, and that he may send the Messiah,
who has been appointed for you—even Jesus. Heaven
must receive him until the time comes for God to re-
store everything, as he promised long ago through his
holy prophets. For Moses said, 'The Lord your God
will raise up for you a prophet like me from among
your own people; you must listen to everything he
tells you.'"

ROMANS 1:20

For since the creation of the world God's invisible qualities—his eternal power and divine nature—have been clearly seen, being understood from what has been made, so that people are without excuse.

HEBREWS 1:1–3

In the past God spoke to our ancestors through the prophets at many times and in various ways, but in these last days he has spoken to us by his Son, whom he appointed heir of all things, and through whom also he made the universe. The Son is the radiance of God's glory and the exact representation of his being, sustaining all things by his powerful word. After he had provided purification for sins, he sat down at the right hand of the Majesty in heaven.

MEDITATION

Despite what anyone may think or feel, despite what we might think at times, God is not silent. Throughout history, he has used whatever it took to reach the ears of the people he loved. He spoke to Moses on a mountain so people would know how to live. He spoke to Elijah in a still small voice to tell him that he was not alone and that his mission was not completed. He spoke to Ezekiel through a vision so that Ezekiel would not fail to tell his exiled people that God could go anywhere. He spoke through dreams and visions and visitations, through angels, through a donkey, through his law. He spoke volumes through the prophets, who each received a certain measure of the revelation of God.

But their revelation was incomplete. So God sent his only Son, in the flesh, to live among the people and teach them. Jesus, the Son of God, is the "image of the invisible God, the firstborn over all creation" (Colossians 1:15), "the radiance of God's glory" (Hebrews 1:3). Jesus did not just speak about God or for God (as the prophets had). He spoke as God. The entire universe belonged to a tiny baby in a manger who would grow up and speak the most important words we would ever hear. No wonder we failed to understand. But now that we do, we must do as Moses commanded: When he comes, we must listen to everything he tells us.

PRAYER

Holy Son of the living God, Scripture written prior to your incarnation pointed directly to you and your work. You are the fulfillment of those prophecies, the Savior of the world. Prophecies still to be fulfilled are those of your return, when you come to judge the world and rule in righteousness. As I study the Scriptures, open my eyes and my heart and allow me to see you in every page and understand the wisdom in your Word. Help me each day to follow you. In your holy name I pray. Amen.   ✤

day23

COLOSSIANS 1:15–23

The Son is the image of the invisible God, the firstborn over all creation. For in him all things were created: things in heaven and on earth, visible and invisible, whether thrones or powers or rulers or authorities; all things have been created through him and for him. He is before all things, and in him all things hold together. And he is the head of the body, the church; he is the beginning and the firstborn from among the dead, so that in everything he might have the supremacy. For God was pleased to have all his fullness dwell in him, and through him to reconcile to himself all things, whether things on earth or things in heaven, by making peace through his blood, shed on the cross.

Once you were alienated from God and were enemies in your minds because of your evil behavior. But now he has reconciled you by Christ's physical body through death to present you holy in his sight, without blemish and free from accusation — if you continue in your faith, established and firm, and do not move from the hope held out in the gospel.

GALATIANS 4:4–7

But when the set time had fully come, God sent his Son, born of a woman, born under the law, to redeem those under the law, that we might receive adoption to sonship. Because you are his sons, God sent the Spirit of his Son into our hearts, the Spirit who calls out, "*Abba*, Father." So you are no longer a slave, but God's child; and since you are his child, God has made you also an heir.

ROMANS 8:14–17

For those who are led by the Spirit of God are the children of God. The Spirit you received does not make you slaves, so that you live in fear again; rather, the Spirit you received brought about your adoption to sonship. And by him we cry, "*Abba*, Father." The Spirit himself testifies with our spirit that we are God's children. Now if we are children, then we are heirs—heirs of God and co-heirs with Christ, if indeed we share in his sufferings in order that we may also share in his glory.

1 JOHN 3:1–2

See what great love the Father has lavished on us, that we should be called children of God! And that is what we are!… We know that when Christ appears, we shall be like him, for we shall see him as he is.

MEDITATION

We are about to celebrate the birth of the Son of God, the firstborn over all creation—not the first created being, as some religions falsely claim, but the one who holds our universe together and without whom we would have neither life nor breath. His birth in Bethlehem has implications for all of us. Jesus was born on earth so that we could become

God's children too, all of us. The gospel Jesus brought was for everyone, then and now. It destroyed all barriers among people: social, racial and gender-related. Our unity is based on our new identity as children of God. That is what we are! Our status in Christ far surpasses any earthly advantages we would have over one another. There is no room for pride. No distinction of slave or free, no wealthy or poor, no in or out.

We are all God's children. He has sent the Holy Spirit to be within us. We can "hear" God speak to us through His Word. We can speak directly to him in daily prayers. He hears the cries of his children, "*Abba*, Father." All this is our Christmas gift from him. It's a free gift. We cannot earn it. We cannot work for it. All we need to do is accept the gift. God loves us and wants us to be with him, to love him. He accepts us as we are. He has a plan for each one of us. He wants us to be close to him for all eternity. God sent his Son to earth, the baby whose birth brings us Christmas, to make that happen.

PRAYER

Abba, Father, how comforting it is to come to you, knowing your love is a gift I did not earn and can never lose. Thank you. I am in awe as I realize how great a gift this truly is. Though I live in a culture that erects barriers between people, barriers that divide us and make us feel either arrogant or inferior, I am so grateful to you for sending your Son, the Lord Jesus, who broke through these walls with his love, acceptance, forgiveness and service to the lost, to the least and to the lonely. Teach me to treasure all the people I encounter today, to love them and to seek only good for them. In your Son's name I pray. Amen. ❖

day24

MATTHEW 12:15–17

Jesus withdrew from that place. A large crowd followed him, and he healed all who were ill. He warned them not to tell others about him. This was to fulfill what was spoken through the prophet Isaiah.

MATTHEW 16:16

Simon Peter answered, "You are the Messiah, the Son of the living God."

MATTHEW 17:5

While he was still speaking, a bright cloud covered them, and a voice from the cloud said, "This is my Son, whom I love; with him I am well pleased. Listen to him!"

LUKE 4:16–21

He went to Nazareth, where he had been brought up, and on the Sabbath day he went into the synagogue, as was his custom. He stood up to read, and the scroll of the prophet Isaiah was handed to him. Unrolling it, he found the place where it is written:

"The Spirit of the Lord is on me,
    because he has anointed me
    to proclaim good news to the poor.
He has sent me to proclaim freedom for the
        prisoners
    and recovery of sight for the blind,

to set the oppressed free,
to proclaim the year of the Lord's favor."

Then he rolled up the scroll, gave it back to the attendant and sat down. The eyes of everyone in the synagogue were fastened on him. He began by saying to them, "Today this scripture is fulfilled in your hearing."

LUKE 20:9–13

He went on to tell the people this parable: "A man planted a vineyard, rented it to some farmers and went away for a long time. At harvest time he sent a servant to the tenants so they would give him some of the fruit of the vineyard. But the tenants beat him and sent him away empty-handed. He sent another servant, but that one also they beat and treated shamefully and sent away empty-handed. He sent still a third, and they wounded him and threw him out. Then the owner of the vineyard said, 'What shall I do? I will send my son, whom I love; perhaps they will respect him.'"

GALATIANS 4:4–7

But when the set time had fully come, God sent his Son, born of a woman, born under the law, to redeem those under the law, that we might receive adoption to sonship. Because you are his sons, God sent the Spirit of his Son into our hearts, the Spirit who calls out, "*Abba*, Father." So you are no longer a slave, but God's child; and since you are his child, God has made you also an heir.

MEDITATION

It is clear from Scripture that Mary knew her baby was no ordinary boy. An angel told Mary that she would become the mother of the Son of God. It is doubtful that she knew exactly what this meant. Who could have? But now we can know, we can understand who he was and the implications of it, through the power of the Word and the Holy Spirit.

Jesus' claims were exclusive. He is God's only begotten Son. He is the one who reveals who God is, what God looks like in the flesh. Jesus' sinless life, his perfect ministry, the truth of all that he said and the life that he modeled for us were all possible because he came straight from God and is God. And if there was ever any cause to doubt his claims, the way he died and the fact that he was raised from death provide proof. Jesus, the only Son of God, was not resuscitated. He was resurrected after death on the cross. He was seen by those who knew him. He could appear and disappear, walk through locked doors, eat and talk and appear as a normal human being, but with the marks of his crucifixion.

He is the only way to God. And we are to follow him. And the way we do this comes from God's own words out of heaven as Jesus was coming up out of the water of his baptism: "Listen to him!"

PRAYER

Lord Jesus, I want to know you better. I want to know more about who you really are and what you are like. Scripture reveals wonderful truths about you. You are the Christ, the

Son of the living God, but my understanding of what that means is so limited. Your majesty and glory are beyond my human comprehension. Grant to me the joy of each day growing in my knowledge of you. In your holy name I pray. Amen. ✢

day25

PHILIPPIANS 2:5–11

In your relationships with one another, have the same mindset as Christ Jesus:

> Who, being in very nature God,
>> did not consider equality with God
>>> something to be used to his own
>>> advantage;
> rather, he made himself nothing
>> by taking the very nature of a servant,
>> being made in human likeness.
> And being found in appearance as a man,
>> he humbled himself
>> by becoming obedient to death—
>>> even death on a cross!
> Therefore God exalted him to the highest place
>> and gave him the name that is above every
>>> name,
> that at the name of Jesus every knee should bow,
>> in heaven and on earth and under the earth,
> and every tongue acknowledge that Jesus
>>> Christ is Lord,
>> to the glory of God the Father.

HEBREWS 2:10–11,14–18

In bringing many sons and daughters to glory, it was fitting that God, for whom and through whom everything exists, should make the pioneer of their salvation perfect through what he suffered. Both the one who makes people holy and those who are made holy are of the same family. So Jesus is not ashamed to call them brothers and sisters.

Since the children have flesh and blood, he too shared in their humanity so that by his death he might break the power of him who holds the power of death—that is, the devil—and free those who all their lives were held in slavery by their fear of death. For surely it is not angels he helps, but Abraham's descendants. For this reason he had to be made like them, fully human in every way, in order that he might become a merciful and faithful high priest in service to God, and that he might make atonement for the sins of the people. Because he himself suffered when he was tempted, he is able to help those who are tempted.

1 THESSALONIANS 3:13

May he strengthen your hearts so that you will be blameless and holy in the presence of our God and Father when our Lord Jesus comes with all his holy ones.

MEDITATION

The first heresy the early church encountered was called Docetism, the idea that because Jesus was God, he could not be fully human and have a human body. Those who believed this heresy believed that because Jesus was God, he only seemed to have a human body and that his death on the cross was not that of a human dying—it only seemed to be the suffering and death of a man. But the writers of the New Testament go to great lengths to make it clear for us: Jesus Christ was both fully God *and* fully human. He was not a superhero sent from another planet. Rather, he was a human being sent to fulfill his Father's agenda. Jesus became like us in every way. And he never succumbed to temptation, thereby falling into the sin and rebellion of humans.

Jesus never sinned. He is a model for us, of how we are to live, setting aside our pride, our ego, our agendas as we submit to the transforming internal work of the Holy Spirit, who dwells in us. In his humility, Christ identified with us for the sake of our redemption. He became one with us in our weakness and modeled complete dependence on the Father. His weakness led him from his birth in a cattle barn to his nighttime flight to Egypt to the inconspicuous village of Nazareth to his itinerant ministry and finally to his death on a Roman cross.

But Jesus overcame the power of death. In three days, as he promised, he rose from the dead. He spent time with his disciples, proving to them that, although he had died and been buried, he was what he said he was—the Son of God. And it is through believing in Jesus, trusting in Jesus, that we too overcome death and are granted eternal life.

PRAYER

Dear God, you have gone to such amazing lengths to make it possible for me to have eternal life through your Son, Jesus Christ. You sent your Son to earth, exchanging the glory and majesty of heaven for the poverty and suffering of earth. Through your amazing grace, you rescued me from this world of sin and hopelessness to a new life with purpose, fellowship, love and hope. Jesus' love has lifted me up. His grace has given me hope. His suffering and death on the cross paid my debt of sin and offered me the glories of eternal life. My salvation is a gift given freely. All I had to do was accept. Thank you for loving me. Guide me, Lord, as I walk in humility in this life with you. I pray, in Jesus' name. Amen. ❖

Once-A-Day Devotional for Women

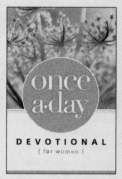

This devotional book is designed with 365 daily readings created specifically for women. Using devotions from Livingstone, the group that produced the *Life Application® Study Bible*, each daily reading includes a Scripture passage to read, a devotion on that passage, a prayer, plus additional Scriptures to explore.

Softcover: 978-0-310-44072-7

Once-A-Day Devotional for Men

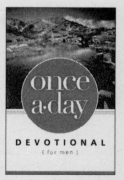

With this *Once-A-Day Devotional for Men*, every day can be spent learning to be more of a man after God's own heart. This devotional book is designed with 365 daily readings created specifically for men. Each daily reading includes a Scripture passage, a devotion on that passage from the trusted team that brought you the *Life Application® Study Bible* notes, and a prayer starter to help lead you into conversation with God.

Softcover: 978-0-310-44074-1

ZONDERVAN®
.com